# EXPLORE ANTARCTICA

**Louise Crossley**

CAMBRIDGE
UNIVERSITY PRESS

AUSTRALIAN ANTARCTIC FOUNDATION

**AUS**LIG AUSTRALIAN SURVEYING & LAND INFORMATION GROUP

Published by the Press Syndicate of the University of Cambridge
The Pitt Building, Trumpington Street, Cambridge CB2 1RP, UK
40 West 20th Street, New York, NY 10011–4211, USA
10 Stamford Road, Oakleigh, Melbourne 3166, Australia

First published 1995
Reprinted in 1997, 1998

Printed in Hong Kong by Colorcraft

*National Library of Australia cataloguing-in-publication data*
Crossley, Louise.
Explore Antarctica.
Includes index.
1. Antarctica. I. Australian Surveying and Land Information Group.
II. Australian Antarctic Foundation. III. Title.
998

*Library of Congress cataloguing-in-publication data*
Crossley, Louise.
Explore Antarctica/Louise Crossley.
   p.   cm.
Includes index.
1. Antarctica–Juvenile literature. [1. Antarctica.] I. Title
G863. C76   1995
919.8'9–dc20                                94–30994
                                                                 CIP
                                                                  AC

*A catalogue record for this book is available from the British Library*

ISBN 0 521 45566 9 Paperback

**Notice to Teachers**

**Acknowledgements**

Cambridge University Press thanks the following staff of the Australian Surveying and Land Information Group (AUSLIG):

    Project coordination — Ruth Dodd
    Design — Ian King
    Desktop publishing — Ian King and Jane Lawson
    Cartography and graphics — Alyx Russell, John Knight and Geoff Grimmett

AUSLIG and Cambridge University Press acknowledge the substantial support provided by the Australian Antarctic Foundation, Department of Foreign Affairs and Trade.

The author warmly acknowledges Dr Pat Quilty's role as Scientific Adviser, and the advice, assistance and information contributed by the following organisations and individuals in the preparation of this book:

    *Australian Antarctic Division*: Evelyn Barrett, Kevin Bell, Rob Easther, Knowles Kerry,
        Harvey Marchant, Ray Price, Graham Robertson, Rod Seppelt,
        Rupert Summerson, Rene Wanless, Dick Williams
    *Australian Geological Survey Organisation*: Bob Tingey, Elizabeth Truswell
    *Australian National University*: John Handmer, Nigel Wace
    *Bureau of Meteorology*: Hugh Hutchinson, Ian Barnes Kegan, Paul Lehmann
    *Commission for the Conservation of Antarctic Marine Living Resources*: Darry Powell,
        Esteban de Salas
    *Commonwealth Scientific and Industrial Research Organisation*: John Church,
        Penelope Greenslade, Peter Shaughnessy
    *University of Sydney*: Michael Bryden
    *University of Tasmania*: Ian Allison, Bruce Davis, Marc Duldig, Jo Jacka

# FOREWORD

If any nation should know about and care for Antarctica it is surely Australia. Chile and Argentina apart, we are the closest of the world's nations to that great frozen continent and as it happens we have claimed more of it than any other nation, no less than 42% of the continent. More importantly, Australia has long been involved in its exploration ever since the heroic pioneering work of Sir Douglas Mawson. Then too, Australia was a foundation member of the Antarctic Treaty System and has been prominent in its development and in the struggle to protect the fragile environment of the continent. At its Antarctic bases Australian scientists, in cooperation with those of other nations, do field work and research of great value to humanity.

If all these are some of the good reasons for not only Australians, but all people of the world to be aware of the great southern continent, it is books such as this that make it possible for young people to be more than merely aware, to instead learn all they should about Antarctica.

The magical thing that so many have discovered about the Antarctic is that the more you learn about it the greater is the fascination it has for you. This is the same effect as is felt by those who visit the continent; they return to civilisation with a new perspective and, very often, with a determination, whatever the cost, to revisit that harsh yet beautiful continent.

I hope that this book will give its readers some sense of the fascination that Antarctica has for those that know it. In doing so, it will have enriched their lives.

THE RT. HON. SIR NINIAN STEPHEN
Chairman, Australian Antarctic Foundation

# PREFACE

*Explore Antarctica*! What a challenge!

Antarctica is the most remote and mysterious continent on earth, a continent of the imagination as well as a vast icy wilderness. One writer has described Antarctica as a 'white hole', an energy and information sink similar to the black holes in space. And like space travel, exploring Antarctica has an enduring fascination for poets, artists and writers as well as scientists and travellers.

Its challenges are diverse. Still perhaps the greatest is the physical challenge of first getting there, and then surviving and getting about in such an extreme environment. Even though there is now centrally heated accommodation at the South Pole, outside this cocoon people still face the same physical dangers as Scott or Amundsen. And even with modern technology and communications, Antarctica still provides people with a psychological and social challenge in living and working with others from different nations or backgrounds in isolated and stressful conditions.

But despite its hardships, Antarctica is an exhilarating environment. The grandeur of its landscape challenges our aesthetic sense, while the wonder of its wildlife and the glory of its auroras can evoke an intense emotional response. Those who experience not just the spectacular beauty of the fringes of the continent but the awesome emptiness of the interior, may confront a profound spiritual challenge.

Antarctica also challenges our scientific understanding with some of the most complex problems of the past and of the future of our planet. Within and beneath its icy mantle, Antarctica holds the key to many secrets, from the structure of the ancient supercontinent of Gondwana to the impact of global warming.

The most fundamental challenge we confront in Antarctica is how to live in peace and harmony with our fellow human beings, and all the species with which we share the planet. The international treaty which governs Antarctica has so far protected the continent from war and its environment from exploitation. Can we build on this inspiration, and the inspiration of Antarctica's unique physical grandeur, to create a new perspective on humanity's relationship with the Earth, which could be the key to the long-term survival of our society and our species?

I hope that *Explore Antarctica* will enable readers to experience the fascination and to appreciate the challenges of this unique continent.

Louise Crossley

# CONTENTS

# Explore Antarctica

ANTARCTICA is a continent like no other. Ninety-eight percent of it is covered in a permanent ice sheet, where howling blizzards, freezing temperatures and months of darkness make life for its few inhabitants an eternal battle for survival. It is surrounded by the stormiest ocean in the world which, unlike the barren continent, is teeming with rich and varied life.

## Untamed wilderness

*The map below shows that only the fringes of Antarctica are inhabited by people, and even those very sparsely. From the coast, the ice sheet rises towards the centre, much of it never explored on the ground.*

This untamed land was a daunting challenge to explorers who strove for decades to reach the spot which defines the South Pole. Now, the ice may hold answers to the puzzle of global warming, auroras can help unravel the mysteries of outer space, and the bounty of the Southern Ocean could help feed the world.

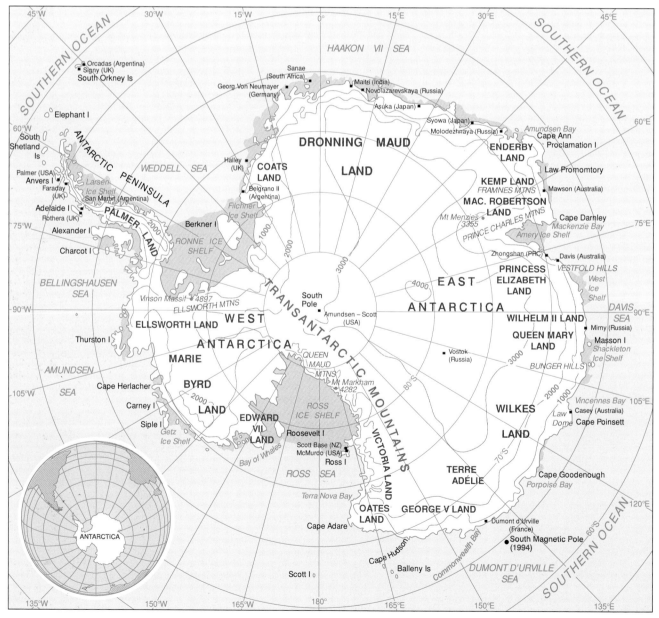

## A unique continent

No one who visits Antarctica comes away unchanged. The beauty of its amazing wildlife, its constantly changing light, and the many shapes and colours of its ice, are overwhelming. Isolation, hardship and danger bind people into a special relationship with each other and with the landscape.

Antarctica has a unique system of government. No one owns it, although seven nations claim parts of it. An international treaty gives all countries the right to explore its scientific mysteries, but none the right to exploit its resources. It is defined as a natural reserve devoted to peace and science.

## Past, present and future

*Explore Antarctica* encourages you to appreciate the past, understand the present and help to ensure that Antarctica's future continues to inspire and inform us about how to live with each other and with the planet.

*This satellite image conveys the beauty and mystery of Antarctica, which has fascinated people for centuries.*

# Antarctica today

A NTARCTICA is the fifth largest continent in the world and covers 10% of the earth's land surface. Like Australia, it is an island continent, but in all other ways it is very different.

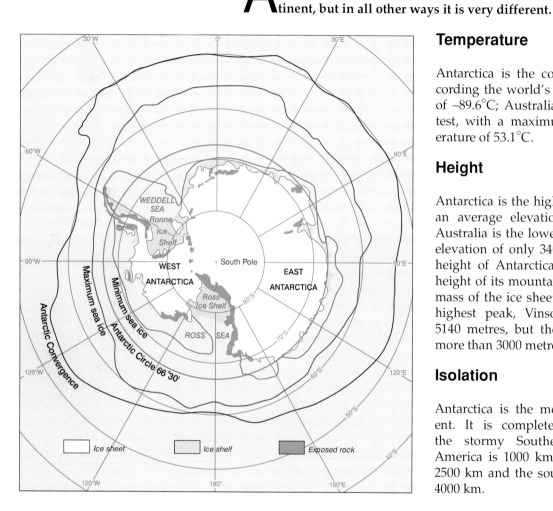

## Temperature

Antarctica is the coldest continent, recording the world's lowest temperature of –89.6°C; Australia is one of the hottest, with a maximum recorded temperature of 53.1°C.

## Height

Antarctica is the highest continent, with an average elevation of 2300 metres; Australia is the lowest, with an average elevation of only 340 metres. The great height of Antarctica is not due to the height of its mountains, but to the huge mass of the ice sheet that covers it. The highest peak, Vinson Massif, is only 5140 metres, but the ice sheet rises to more than 3000 metres over a large area.

## Isolation

Antarctica is the most isolated continent. It is completely surrounded by the stormy Southern Ocean. South America is 1000 km away, Australia is 2500 km and the southern tip of Africa 4000 km.

## Size

Antarctica is roughly circular, with a diameter of about 4500 km, a circumference of 32 000 km, and an area of nearly 14 million km², which is almost twice as big as Australia. A permanent ice sheet (☛ p. 22) covering the continental rock makes up 87% of this area; 11% is permanent floating ice

This diagram (right) shows a section through the continent from A to B. The ice sheet is much higher in East Antarctica than West Antarctica. Most of the land is below sea level, due to the weight of ice on top.

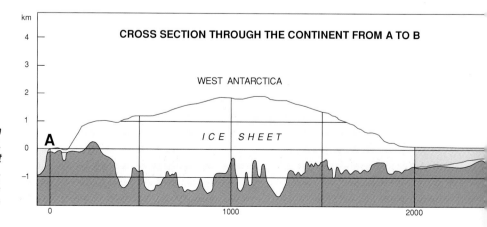

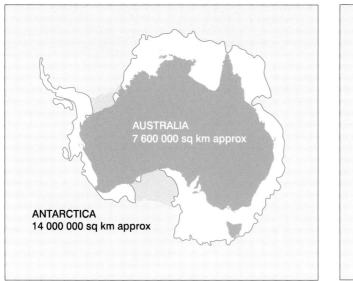

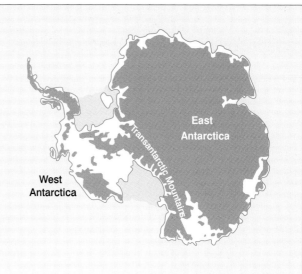

*Antarctica is nearly twice the size of Australia (left). If all the ice was removed (above), the land would rise and East Antarctica would be a continent about the size of Australia, while West Antarctica would be a collection of islands.*

shelves (☛ p. 24); and only 2% is exposed rock (☛ p. 14). In winter the ice-covered area more than doubles, with the surface of the ocean freezing for as much as 1000 km from the coast over an area of 20 million km$^2$ (☛ p. 26).

## Antarctic Convergence

The influence of Antarctica extends even further north into the Southern Ocean than this, however, to a zone known as the Antarctic Convergence. This is the zone where cold dense water from the Antarctic meets warmer, less dense water in the subtropical region of the ocean. Across this zone, which is about 40 km wide, the sea surface temperature changes by about 2°C (☛ p. 54). The Convergence is a roughly circular boundary which shifts with the seasons, but it is usually at around 58°S.

## East and West Antarctica

Antarctica can be divided into two quite different regions. East or Greater Antarctica makes up two-thirds of the area of the continent and contains 88% of the ice sheet. Below, it is a single, ancient landmass (☛ p. 15), bounded by the Transantarctic Mountains stretching nearly 5000 km from the Ross Sea to the Weddell Sea. West, or Lesser, Antarctica is much smaller and lower, although it contains the highest mountain peak. Below its ice sheet are a number of separate land masses which would become islands if the ice was removed.

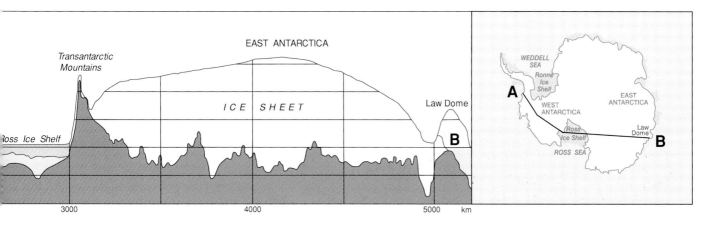

# Antarctica in the past

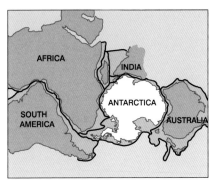

Geologists have reconstructed Gondwana, and find that the shapes of the continental shelves at the 1000 metre line fit very closely.

**470 Ma**
Antarctica was near the equator and locked into the jigsaw of Gondwana, surrounded on three sides by Australia, India, Africa and the tip of South America.

**280 Ma**
Antarctica had slid southwards and was over the South Pole. A major ice age occurred on the southern continents — Antarctica, Australia, India, Africa and South America.

ANTARCTICA has not always been at the South Pole, and it has not always been a separate continent. It has a long and complex geological history which scientists are still trying to piece together.

However, the main pieces of the jigsaw are now fairly well established. Until about 160 million years ago (Ma), Antarctica was part of a supercontinent called Gondwana, which also included Australasia, Africa, South

*Antarctica sits almost in the middle of its own tectonic plate, joined on to the other five main southern hemisphere plates which are still moving away from it.*

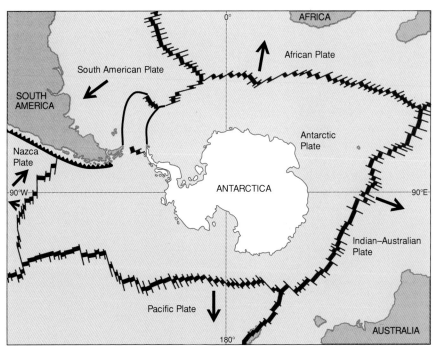

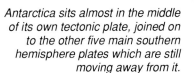

Subduction zone

Collision zone

Spreading ridge with transform faults

Direction of movement of plates

## Geological time scale

| Age    (Ma) | 3600 – 2500 | 2500 – 1800 | 1800 – 1000 | 1000 – 570 | 570 – 500 | 500 – 435 | 435 – 410 |
|---|---|---|---|---|---|---|---|
| Period | Archaean | Early Proterozoic | Middle Proterozoic | Late Proterozoic | Cambrian | Ordovician | Silurian |
| Era | Archaean | Proterozoic | | | | Palaeozoic | |
| Eon | PRECAMBRIAN | | | | | | |

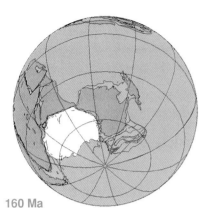

**160 Ma**
*This was a warm period with no polar ice caps. Antarctica had shifted away from the South Pole, as a prelude to the break-up of Gondwana.*

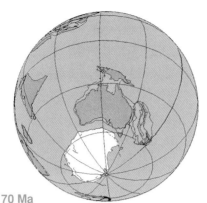

**70 Ma**
*Antarctica moved back close to the South Pole, and wide oceans developed between Antarctica, and Africa and India. A new ocean opened between Antarctica and Australia, and the Tasman Sea formed between Australia and New Zealand.*

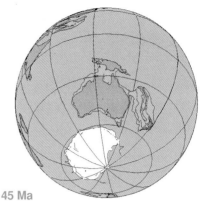

**45 Ma**
*Antarctica continued to shift towards the South Pole, and became surrounded by oceans as Australia headed north. The encircling oceans isolated Antarctica and gradually cooled it.*

America and India. Over the next 100 million years, Gondwana broke up, and the individual continents moved apart to their present positions.

## Plate tectonics

Scientists explain these movements by the theory of plate tectonics. The surface of the earth consists of a series of plates which can move around on the earth's molten core. Different continents ride on these plates. Where they collide, volcanic activity is common. Where they pull apart, ocean floors and rift valleys form. The supercontinent of Gondwana as a whole also moved around the globe, so Antarctica's climate changed as a result.

## Fossil evidence

Fossils of a number of plants found in Antarctica show it was once much warmer. One deciduous conifer called *Glossopteris* occurs in both East and West Antarctica. Similar fossils of the same age have been found in Africa, South America, Australia and India. Fossil remains of a land reptile called *Lystrosaurus* have also been found both in Antarctica and other continents now widely separated from it. Neither *Lystrosaurus* nor *Glossopteris* could cross oceans. These fossils suggest that Antarctica and the other continents where they are found were once joined together.

One of the biggest puzzles remaining is the relationship between East and West Antarctica. Below the icy mantle which now unites them, they have very different geological origins. East Antarctica is a very old landmass which formed the core of Gondwana as it moved around the globe. West Antarctica is made up of several pieces of different ages which seem to have moved into place quite independently.

Glossopteris *fossils show that Antarctica has been much warmer than it is now.*

| 410 – 345 | 345 – 300 | 300 – 235 | 235 – 195 | 195 – 135 | 135 – 65 | 65 – 2 | 2 – Present |
|---|---|---|---|---|---|---|---|
| Devonian | Carboniferous | Permian | Triassic | Jurassic | Cretaceous | Tertiary | Quaternary |
| | | | | Mesozoic | | Cainozoic | |
| PHANEROZOIC | | | | | | | |

# Antarctica's changing climate

## The last 1000 million years

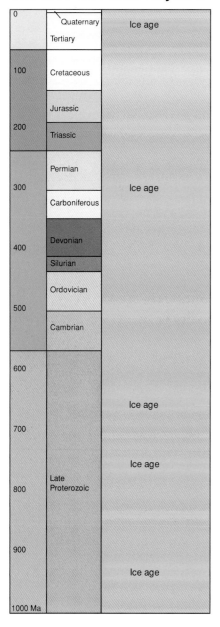

| | | |
|---|---|---|
| 0 | Quaternary | Ice age |
| | Tertiary | |
| 100 | Cretaceous | |
| | Jurassic | |
| 200 | Triassic | |
| | Permian | |
| 300 | Carboniferous | Ice age |
| 400 | Devonian | |
| | Silurian | |
| | Ordovician | |
| 500 | Cambrian | |
| 600 | | |
| | | Ice age |
| 700 | | |
| | | Ice age |
| 800 | Late Proterozoic | |
| 900 | | Ice age |
| 1000 Ma | | |

THE climate of Antarctica has varied from subtropical to freezing through a series of cycles of different lengths over the last 2000 million years. Some of these cycles were related to global ice ages resulting from changes in the earth's orbit around the sun.

One of these global ice ages occurred in the early Precambrian period of the earth's geological evolution around 2000 Ma (☛ p. 10). This was followed by other ice ages around 940 Ma, 770 Ma and 660 Ma, in the later part of the Precambrian period.

## Tropical Antarctica

During the Cambrian period, around 500 Ma, Antarctica was in the tropics and at its warmest ever. The next major ice age was in the late Carboniferous and Permian period around 320–260 Ma.

From the time of the break-up of Gondwana, Antarctica has remained in about its present position over the South Pole. When Australia and Antarctica separated, the continent was very warm, and the surrounding Southern Ocean was also still quite warm, about 18°–20°C.

## Antarctica cools down

By about 45 Ma the waters of the Southern Ocean had cooled to 12°–13°C, and temperatures on the continent also fell. During that period Antarctica was covered with ancient forerunners of the modern southern cold temperate rainforests of Tasmania, New Zealand and South America. Trees similar to the *Nothofagus gunnii*, or Antarctic beech, which is found in Tasmania today, still grew widely across Antarctica up to 30 Ma. However, this represents only a very small period in the overall climatic history of Antarctica.

The main reason for the cooling of Antarctica was the opening of the gap between Tasmania and East Antarctica, and of Drake Passage between South America and the Antarctic Peninsula. This created a deep-water cir-

*The beautiful colours of* Nothofagus gunnii, *or Antarctic beech, once covered much of Antarctica.*

*Coal seams near Beaver Lake in the Prince Charles Mountains show there were lots of trees here about 200 Ma.*

culation in the Southern Ocean around the continent, which cut it off from the warming influence of subtropical waters. The East Antarctic ice sheet grew to about its present size by 15 Ma, although West Antarctica still only had a series of large glaciers rather than a complete ice cap.

## Climate cycles

Even since then, however, there is evidence of great variations in the climate, which scientists still do not fully understand. Sediments from the ocean floor suggest that warmer water organisms were living in the Southern Ocean around 10 Ma and again at 8 Ma. So the climate of the continent may have been warmer then as well. Fossil dolphins dating from around 4.2–3.5 Ma have been found many kilometres inland near Australia's Davis station. This suggests that at that time warm water covered this area, and the sea level was higher due to melting of the ice sheet. Fossils of *Nothofagus* dating from 3–2.5 Ma have been found in the Transantarctic Mountains. This indicates that some remnants of earlier forests had survived, and became more widespread when the climate warmed up again around then.

From around 2.5 Ma, the Antarctic ice sheet probably took on its present form. Since then, however, there have been global cycles of glaciation which also affected Antarctica.

## The last ice age

There is evidence that in the last glacial maximum only 18 000 years ago, the ice sheet was as much as 100–500 metres higher in different parts of the continent. Moraines stranded high on the sides of mountains above the present ice sheet indicate that glaciers once flowed past at that level, and dropped the rocks they were carrying at the sides of the stream.

The evidence from ice cores (☛ p. 104) covering the last 160 000 years also shows cycles of warming and cooling. It is important for scientists to understand as much as possible about these natural variations in Antarctica's climate, as a basis for predicting the possible impact of variations caused by human actions such as the 'Greenhouse effect' (☛ pp. 100–106).

## The last 50 million years

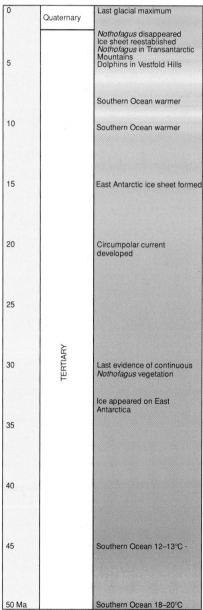

| Ma | Period | Event |
|----|--------|-------|
| 0 | Quaternary | Last glacial maximum |
| 5 | | *Nothofagus* disappeared<br>Ice sheet reestablished<br>*Nothofagus* in Transantarctic Mountains<br>Dolphins in Vestfold Hills |
| | | Southern Ocean warmer |
| 10 | | Southern Ocean warmer |
| 15 | | East Antarctic ice sheet formed |
| 20 | | Circumpolar current developed |
| 25 | | |
| 30 | TERTIARY | Last evidence of continuous *Nothofagus* vegetation |
| 35 | | Ice appeared on East Antarctica |
| 40 | | |
| 45 | | Southern Ocean 12–13°C |
| 50 Ma | | Southern Ocean 18–20°C |

# Skeleton and structure

F OR most of its geological history, Antarctica has not been covered in ice (☛ p. 12). But as only 2% of the continent is now ice-free, there is little surface evidence from which scientists can piece together its geology.

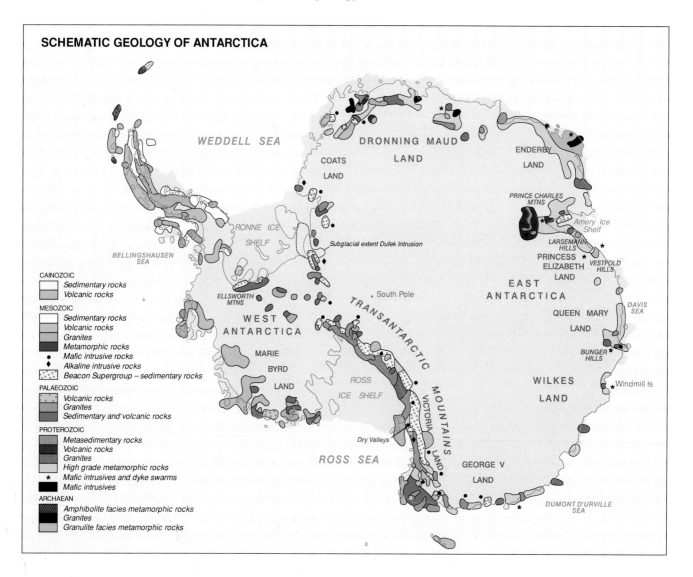

**SCHEMATIC GEOLOGY OF ANTARCTICA**

WEDDELL SEA

DRONNING MAUD LAND

COATS LAND

ENDERBY LAND

PRINCE CHARLES MTNS

Amery Ice Shelf

RONNE ICE SHELF

Subglacial extent Dufek Intrusion

LARSEMANN HILLS

PRINCESS ELIZABETH LAND

VESTFOLD HILLS

BELLINGSHAUSEN SEA

EAST ANTARCTICA

DAVIS SEA

ELLSWORTH MTNS

South Pole

QUEEN MARY LAND

WEST ANTARCTICA

TRANSANTARCTIC MOUNTAINS

BUNGER HILLS

MARIE BYRD LAND

ROSS ICE SHELF

VICTORIA LAND

WILKES LAND

Windmill Is

Dry Valleys

ROSS SEA

GEORGE V LAND

DUMONT D'URVILLE SEA

CAINOZOIC
- Sedimentary rocks
- Volcanic rocks

MESOZOIC
- Sedimentary rocks
- Volcanic rocks
- Granites
- Metamorphic rocks
- • Mafic intrusive rocks
- ♦ Alkaline intrusive rocks
- Beacon Supergroup – sedimentary rocks

PALAEOZOIC
- Volcanic rocks
- Granites
- Sedimentary and volcanic rocks

PROTEROZOIC
- Metasedimentary rocks
- Volcanic rocks
- Granites
- High grade metamorphic rocks
- ✶ Mafic intrusives and dyke swarms
- Mafic intrusives

ARCHAEAN
- Amphibolite facies metamorphic rocks
- Granites
- Granulite facies metamorphic rocks

## Geological evidence

Most information comes from the ice-free 'oases', of which the largest are the Dry Valleys in Victoria Land, the Bunger Hills in Queen Mary Land, and the Vestfold and Larsemann Hills in Princess Elizabeth Land. Where mountain ranges such as the Transantarctic and Prince Charles Mountains in East Antarctica and the Ellsworth Mountains in West Antarctica pierce the ice sheet, there are also exposed rocks.

Geologists also use seismic techniques, which send shock waves through the rock layers beneath the ice, to measure the thickness of the crust. Melting icebergs drop about 500 million tonnes of rock and sediment on the sea floor each year, and drill cores of these deposits can also yield useful information.

## East and West

From these scattered sources, geologists have built up a picture of the geological structure and history of Antarctica. East Antarctica is underlain by an ancient landmass 40–50 km thick, dating from around 3800 Ma, and this is covered by younger rocks.

The Transantarctic Mountains, which form the boundary between East and West Antarctica, reveal a complicated historical sequence of uplift, folding and erosion of several layers of rocks. The present mountain range was uplifted about 30 Ma and then buried by the growing ice sheet from 15 Ma onwards, until now only the peaks show above it.

West Antarctica is made up of several smaller continental blocks which would be islands if the ice was removed (☞ p. 9). They are only about 30 km thick and were formed around 200–150 Ma, probably through the buckling of the Antarctic plate at its boundary with the South American plate during the break-up of Gondwana (☞ pp. 10–11).

## The Dry Valleys

The Dry Valleys and other oases are unique to Antarctica. They are all close to the coast, and are formed by the retreat of local glaciers. The 3000 km² Dry Valleys of Victoria Land resulted from uplift of the Transan-

*Only the peaks of the Transantarctic Mountains emerge above the ice sheet.*

tarctic Mountains at a faster rate than the glaciers were able to cut their way down through the valleys. Eventually the glaciers became trapped behind a rock lip at the head of the valleys. Once this happened, dry winds kept the valleys free of snow, and a unique micro-climate was established where no rain has fallen for the last 2 million years. This cold, rocky desert is the closest thing to Mars on earth, and NASA has sent astronauts there for training in extra-terrestrial living.

Other reminders of outer space are also found in Antarctica — in the form of meteorite fragments. When they fall on Antarctica, meteorites are trapped in the ice, moving with it towards the coast and usually floating away in icebergs. But in some places, where the ice flow comes up against a barrier like a mountain ridge, the wind scours away the ice and the meteorites are brought to the surface. In one area like this near the Dry Valleys, over 5000 meteorite fragments have been found in the last 20 years, adding much to our knowledge of other parts of our galaxy.

*Rocks fall and are scoured from mountains onto the glaciers and form a moraine 'tail'.*

## Weather 1: Antarctica and world weather

ANTARCTICA and the Southern Ocean are key elements in the global weather system. This is a system which creates and transfers energy as winds, clouds, rain and all the other elements we call 'the weather'.

### Atmospheric circulation

The source of this energy is the sun, and because its heating effect is greater at the equator than at the poles, it creates a circulation in the atmosphere. Hot, moist air rises over the equator and flows at a high level towards the poles, where it cools and sinks. The equator is therefore a region of low pressure, and the poles are regions of high pressure. So the surface flow of air is in the reverse direction, from the poles to the equator. In between are several belts of high and low pressure in each hemisphere. The Southern Ocean is a region of low pressure which produces the westerly winds of the roaring forties, furious fifties and screaming sixties.

### Interaction between atmosphere and ocean

But the atmosphere is not a closed system. It interacts with the land, the ocean and the ice; and the ice in turn interacts with the ocean. For example, winds create currents in the ocean. In addition, the annual cycle of freezing and melting of sea ice around Antarctica (☞ p. 26) creates a vertical circulation in the ocean (☞ p. 54) similar to that in the atmosphere. As a result, there is a massive exchange of heat and energy between the ice, the ocean and the atmosphere. So Antarctica and the Southern Ocean play a major role in the global energy balance, which affects weather around the world.

### Antarctica and Australia

As well as this general influence, the impact of Antarctica and the Southern Ocean on Australia's weather can sometimes be much more dramatic. The satellite picture (left) and weather map (right) below show two low pressure systems funnelling freezing Antarctic air northwards between them, causing a typical 'cold outbreak' over southern Australia.

*The circulation of the atmosphere results from the temperature difference between the equator and the poles. The rotation of the earth causes surface winds to blow around the globe, rather than directly from the poles to the equator.*

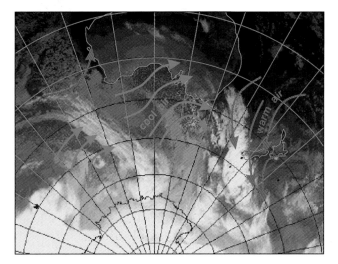

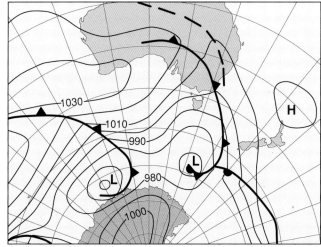

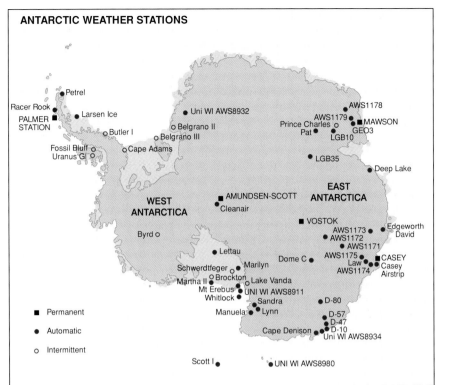

**ANTARCTIC WEATHER STATIONS**

■ Permanent
● Automatic
○ Intermittent

There are 100 weather stations across Antarctica. Most of the staffed ones are on the coast, while automatic stations cover some of the interior.

Automatic weather stations provide data by satellite from inaccessible parts of the continent.

## Weather stations

Because Antarctica's weather is so important to the rest of the world, collecting meteorological information is a major activity of the scientists who work there. There are nearly 100 weather stations on the continent, both staffed and automatic. The data from Australia's stations are sent to the World Meteorological Centre in Melbourne. From there they are distributed to weather forecasting centres around the world. This information also helps scientists developing climate models to test the impact of the 'Greenhouse effect', or to predict cyclones or the El Niño effect.

Information from other parts of the global network is also fed back to the Antarctic Meteorological Centre at Casey. There it is used to provide weather forecasts for operations at Australia's and other nations' bases in Antarctica, and to monitor the formation and break-up of sea ice so that resupply ships can plan their routes to avoid getting trapped.

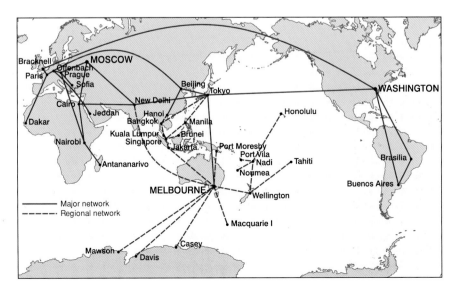

—— Major network
------ Regional network

A meteorological observer releases a hydrogen-filled balloon to measure winds in the upper atmosphere. He wears protective clothing in case the balloon explodes and catches fire.

The data from Antarctica form part of a world-wide network of meteorological information.

# Weather 2: A continent of extremes

**A**NTARCTICA is the coldest continent on earth. It has the coldest average annual temperatures, and the lowest temperature ever recorded was –89.6°C at Vostok on 21 July 1983. There are a number of different reasons which combine to make Antarctica so frigid.

*Antarctica — a continent surrounded by oceans.*

*The Arctic — an ocean surrounded by continents.*

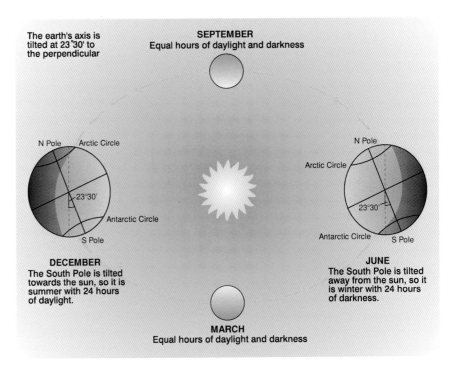

The earth's axis is tilted at 23°30' to the perpendicular

**SEPTEMBER**
Equal hours of daylight and darkness

N Pole   Arctic Circle

23°30'

Antarctic Circle

S Pole

**DECEMBER**
The South Pole is tilted towards the sun, so it is summer with 24 hours of daylight.

N Pole

Arctic Circle

23°30'

Antarctic Circle

S Pole

**JUNE**
The South Pole is tilted away from the sun, so it is winter with 24 hours of darkness.

**MARCH**
Equal hours of daylight and darkness

## Less solar energy

First, the sun doesn't shine at the South Pole for half the year. This is because of the tilt of the earth's axis relative to its orbit around the sun. Second, because of this tilt the sun's rays are much more slanted at the Poles than at the equator. So the same amount of solar energy is spread over a wider area, and since it also passes through a thicker layer of the atmosphere than at the equator, much less actually reaches the ground. Third, when it does reach the ground, most is reflected back into space by the ice and snow covering Antarctica.

*Mean surface temperatures in January and July — it is coldest where it is highest.*

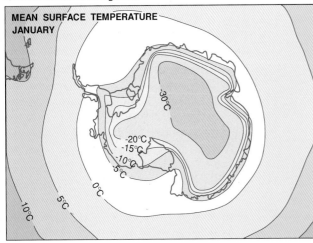

MEAN SURFACE TEMPERATURE
JANUARY

-30°C
-20°C
-15°C
-10°C
-5°C
0°C
5°C
10°C

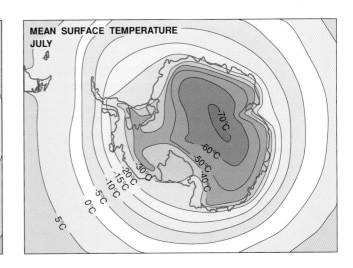

MEAN SURFACE TEMPERATURE
JULY

-70°C
-60°C
-50°C
-40°C
-30°C
-20°C
-15°C
-10°C
-5°C
0°C
5°C

As a result, the continent loses more solar energy than it receives during the year. Only for a short time at midsummer is there a net energy gain.

To make up for this loss, Antarctica has to gain energy from elsewhere. Warmer, moist air rises over the tropics and Southern Ocean and is carried towards the polar plateau, where it condenses and loses its heat. This transfer of warm air from the tropics to the poles is vital in maintaining the heat balance of the whole planet (☛ p. 16).

## Antarctica is colder than the Arctic

Antarctica is colder than the Arctic because it is a continent surrounded by oceans, whereas the Arctic is an ocean surrounded by continents. The belt of westerly winds sweeping round the Southern Ocean isolates Antarctica from the rest of the world and reduces the energy transfer just described. In addition, the southern fringe of the Arctic sea ice thaws in summer, allowing the ocean to absorb more solar radiation, which then acts as a heat source in winter.

## Antarctica's two seasons

Antarctica has only two seasons, a long, uniformly cold winter and a very brief summer. In between, the temperature rises rapidly from September as the sun returns, then plunges equally swiftly as it disappears again in March.

## The South Pole is not the coldest place

The minimum temperature and the annual temperature range vary with latitude and altitude. Although it is the furthest south, the Pole is not the coldest place because at 2800 metres it is not the highest. Vostok at 78°S and 3500 metres has an average temperature of –55°C, with an annual range of about 65°C. At a coastal station like Mawson both these figures are less than half.

Like most places, Antarctica is windier in winter than summer, and windier and wetter on the coast than inland. The high plateau of Antarctica is the world's largest and driest desert. Annual snowfall is equivalent to rainfall of 50 mm — or about half the average rainfall of Birdsville or Oodnadatta.

*In winter, the long night displays the glory of the southern aurora.*

*In summer, the sun sweeps around the horizon without setting.*

**TYPICAL ANTARCTIC WEATHER STATIONS**

| Station | Latitude | Longitude | Height (m) |
|---|---|---|---|
| Amundsen-Scott | 90°S | — | 2800 |
| Vostok | 78°S | 107°E | 3488 |
| Mawson | 68°S | 63°E | 8 |
| Palmer | 65°S | 64°W | 11 |

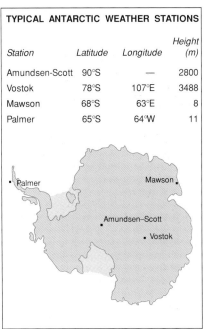

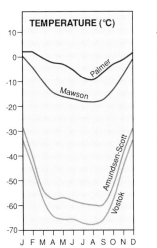

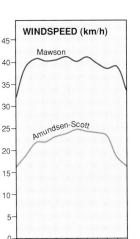

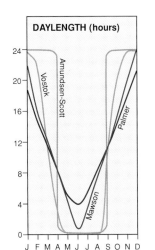

# Weather 3: Continental patterns and special effects

AVERAGE WINDFLOW PATTERN

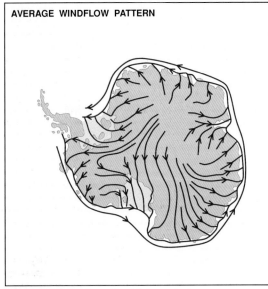

*The wind flows from the high central plateau out towards the coast (above), and is strongest near the coast (below).*

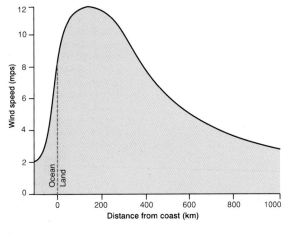

ANTARCTICA is not only the coldest continent on earth — it is also the windiest, partly because it is so cold.

## Katabatic winds

In a warm climate like Australia, the air becomes colder with height above the ground surface. In Antarctica, because it is so cold at the ice surface, this normal pattern is turned upside down, so that the air gets warmer with height instead of colder. This means that on a slope, the air close to the surface is colder and denser than air at the same altitude above a point further down the slope. So this coldest, densest surface layer flows down the slope under gravity, creating a 'katabatic' wind effect.

The whole Antarctic ice sheet is dome shaped, sloping from the centre above 4000 metres out towards the edges at sea level, so air gathers speed as it flows down the slope, just like a stream of water. As a result, the interior of Antarctica is comparatively calm but the coasts are very windy. In general, the wind is strongest about 50 km inland from the coast, and drops away rapidly out to sea. However, where the shape of the ice sheet funnels the wind into a valley, it can blow at gale force for days on end.

## Depressions

Further out in the Southern Ocean constant strong westerly winds create low pressure systems or depressions, which on a typical satellite picture can be seen ringing the continent. These depressions have a life span of two to three days as they spiral in towards the coast, where they usually break up. They bring warmer moist air from the ocean and can cause heavy snowfalls on the steep slopes rising to the plateau.

## Blizzards and whiteout

Wind, cold, snow, ice and cloud make Antarctica's one of the world's most treacherous climates. Snow and wind produce blizzards, which can bring

*Whiteout causes disorientation by destroying a sense of height and distance.*

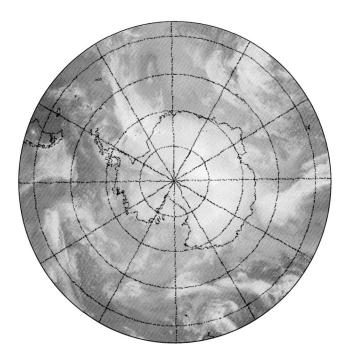
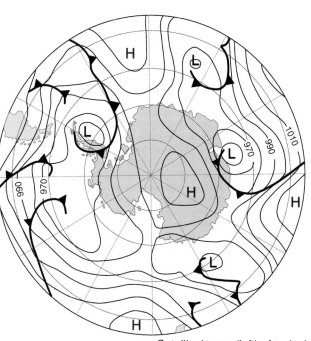

*Satellite image (left) of typical Antarctic weather systems on 8 October 1993 and weather map (right) of the same systems, based on sea level pressures.*

all human activity to a halt, often for several days at a time. The entire atmosphere seems to be full of whirling snow, with winds over 60 km/h and visibility often reduced to less than 10 metres.

Whiteout is almost as dangerous. This is caused by a combination of snow and cloud. The air may be clear, but when the sky is overcast, there are no shadows and no horizon. On a uniformly white snow surface it is impossible to judge height or distance, so that walkers stumble and aircraft and even birds can crash into the snow.

## Windchill

Cold and wind combined are worse than either by itself, because of the windchill effect. The discomfort we feel in the cold depends on the rate at which our bodies lose heat to the air around us. This in turn depends on how cold that air actually is, and how rapidly it is moving past, taking our body heat away. The stronger the wind, the more quickly we lose heat, and the 'colder' we feel. For example, in a 10 km/h wind at –10°C we lose heat as quickly as we would at –70°C in still air. The windchill index (right) is 1200 and so we feel 'bitterly cold'.

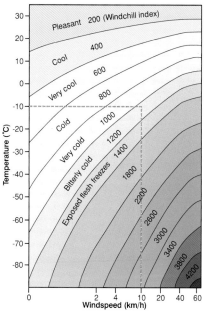

*The windchill index links wind speed and temperature to show equivalent rates of heat loss.*

*'Sundogs' are spectacular Antarctic special effects. They are caused by refraction of the sun's rays by ice crystals in the atmosphere, in much the same way that raindrops cause rainbows in warmer climates.*

# The ice sheet 1: How is it formed?

ANTARCTICA contains 90% of the world's fresh water, locked up in 30 million $km^3$ of ice which covers 98% of the continent. If this amount of ice were spread evenly over Australia, it would form a layer 3 km thick. If it all melted, the sea level world-wide would rise by between 50 and 60 metres.

*Snow crystals*

## How deep is the ice?

Eighty-seven percent or 26 million $km^3$ of this huge volume of ice is in the East Antarctic ice sheet. West Antarctica contains 3.3 million $km^3$, while the rest is in the permanent ice shelves fringing the continent. The greatest thickness of ice in East Antarctica is 4700 metres, half the height of Mt Everest, and the average thickness is 2500–2800 metres. This enormous weight of ice pushes the continental bedrock of East Antarctica below sea level, so the maximum height of the ice sheet is only about 4000 metres (☞ pp. 7-8).

## How is it measured?

Seismic techniques using sound waves (☞ p. 14) were first used to measure the thickness of the ice in specific places. Now sleds carrying radar antennae and pulled by huge tractors can survey many thousands of kilometres. They give a continuous plot of the shape of the bedrock and the height of the ice sheet, allowing very accurate calculations of the depth and surface contours of the ice.

*Drifting snow quickly builds up in the lee of buildings in strong winds.*

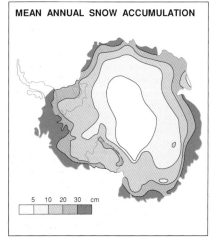

MEAN ANNUAL SNOW ACCUMULATION

5   10   20   30   cm

*The areas of greatest ice thickness (right) are not the same as areas of maximum snow accumulation (above). This shows that the ice sheet has been built up over many millions of years.*

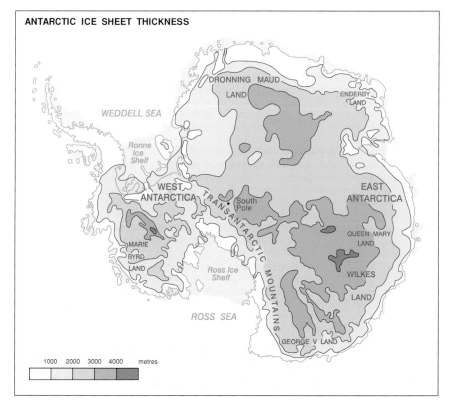

ANTARCTIC ICE SHEET THICKNESS

DRONNING MAUD LAND

ENDERBY LAND

WEDDELL SEA

Ronne Ice Shelf

WEST ANTARCTICA

South Pole

EAST ANTARCTICA

MARIE BYRD LAND

Ross Ice Shelf

QUEEN MARY LAND

WILKES LAND

ROSS SEA

GEORGE V LAND

1000   2000   3000   4000   metres

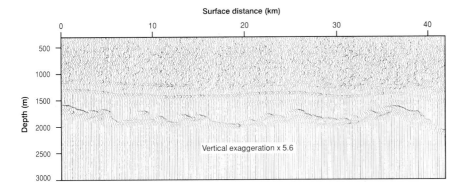

A typical ice radar profile shows a well defined echo from the bedrock at 1500–1800 metres.

## Snow accumulation

The huge mass of the Antarctic ice sheet has accumulated from millions of years of snowfall. Water evaporated from the oceans is carried high into the atmosphere over Antarctica (☞ p. 19) where it forms ice crystals centred on minute particles of dust. Snowflakes grow by the combination of ice crystals into a variety of symmetrical shapes (left) as they fall.

Because the air over Antarctica is so cold, it cannot carry much moisture, even as snow, so very little falls in the centre of the continent. The annual snowfall at the South Pole is equivalent to the rainfall in the Sahara Desert, and only about 2–5 cm of snow accumulates there each year. Snowfall is higher around the coast and more is carried there from inland by the katabatic winds (☞ p. 20), so accumulation can be up to 2 metres a year.

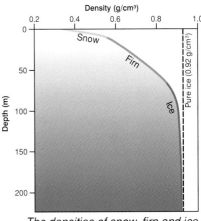

The densities of snow, firn and ice vary with depth.

## Ice formation

As snow accumulates in deeper and deeper layers, it gradually turns into ice. Freshly fallen snow is fluffy and full of air pockets, with a density of only 0.1–0.2 g/cm$^3$. As the layer gets thicker, the complex shapes of the snowflakes are packed more closely into spheres, and the density increases to about 0.55 g/cm$^3$. At this stage the snow has become 'firn'.

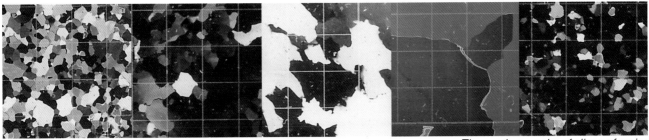

As the depth increases, the spheres are pressed closer together into larger crystals. At around 70–100 metres the packing is so tight that the air gaps between the crystals are closed off, and the firn turns into 'bubbly ice' with a density of 0.82 g/cm$^3$. Deeper still, the crystals merge together and absorb the air trapped between them, until pure ice with a density of 0.92 g/cm$^3$ is formed. At depths of over 1000 metres, the crystals can be as much as 50 mm across.

These micrographs of slices of an ice core taken in polarised light show how the crystal size increases with depth. The deepest slice (far right) is close to the bedrock, where the crystals break down because grit is mixed up in the ice. All micrographs show actual crystal size (from left to right):
190 metres, 5–8 mm crystals
837 metres, 10–20 mm crystals
1089 metres, 30–40 mm crystals
1193 metres, 50–60 mm crystals
1195 metres, 2–5 mm crystals

Because the accumulation rate is so slow, this very deep ice may be many thousands of years old. The air trapped in the ice can tell scientists about the atmosphere at the time the snow from which it is made fell on the surface. This helps research into the 'Greenhouse effect' (☞ pp.104–105 ).

# The ice sheet 2: How does it move?

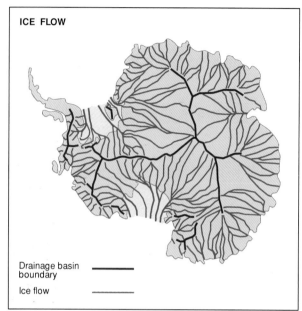

ICE FLOW

Drainage basin
boundary

Ice flow

*The ice sheet flows from the interior to the coast through drainage basins.*

ALTHOUGH the Antarctic ice sheet may have taken millions of years to accumulate, it is not static. Ice is fluid and the ice sheet flows continuously out from the centre to the edges of the continent under the pressure of its own weight, in the same way that icing flows off a cake. The rate of flow varies. It is slowest at the centre and fastest at the edge because the dome-shaped ice sheet slopes more steeply at the edge.

## Drainage systems

The Antarctic ice sheet is divided into five major drainage systems, into which glaciers flow like rivers. Most glaciers flow into ice shelves, the permanent floating slabs of ice that fringe 45% of the coastline. Some glaciers flow directly into the sea, and around the rest of the coast the ice sheet itself forms huge cliffs at the edge of the continent. From these edges, pieces break off as icebergs. The ice sheet loses about 1450 km$^3$ a year in this way.

*The Forbes Glacier near Mawson flows directly into the sea, rather than into an ice shelf.*

*The Battye Glacier is unique in Antarctica, because it flows into a lake, not the sea or an ice shelf. It shows the typical shape of a glacier tongue, floating on the lake, which is also frozen on the surface.*

## How the ice sheet flows

The ice sheet moves in two different ways. First, the whole glacier can slide down its bed under the force of gravity. This can only happen if there is a layer of water between the ice and bedrock to reduce friction. The weight of the ice can be enough to melt the layer next to the bedrock. As a glacier nears the sea, its bed may be below sea level, and so seawater can filter in under the ice to reduce friction. Once it reaches the sea and becomes an ice shelf, it is actually floating and so there is almost no friction.

Second, there is movement within the ice mass itself, caused by the weight of the accumulated snow and ice. Under this pressure, the ice crystals form into layers which slide over each other. Gravity forces these layers to follow the slope within the ice mass, which is steepest at the surface and less steep close to the bedrock. So the glacier does not move as a solid block; rather, the ice moves fastest at the surface and slower near the bedrock.

## Ice cores

Individual ice particles move vertically down through the mass as more accumulates on top, and also along the slope, at different rates at different depths. So individual particles follow curved paths through the ice mass as it flows (right). This also means that an ice core drilled vertically through the ice sheet does not simply contain all the snow and ice that has fallen on that spot over thousands of years. Instead, the deeper in the core the layers are, the further upstream the ice has come from.

## The Lambert Glacier

The Lambert Glacier, the world's largest, demonstrates the typical flow pattern of the ice sheet. It drains an area of over 1 million km$^2$ of East Antarctica, flowing through the Prince Charles Mountains into the Amery Ice Shelf. The glacier is 400 km long and over 40 km wide, and the ice shelf adds another 300 km to its length. On average, 35 km$^3$

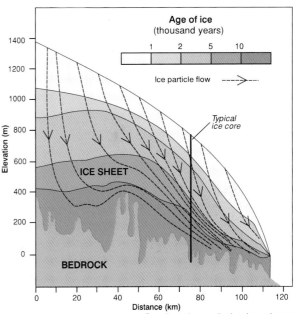

*Section through the ice sheet, showing how ice flows vertically under pressure from accumulation above, and down the slope under gravity. As a result, the age of the ice does not vary evenly with depth.*

of ice a year flows down the glacier and breaks off as icebergs from the ice front, which is 200 km wide where it meets the sea. Through the mountains, the glacier moves at about 230 metres a year, but by the time it reaches the floating ice shelf it has speeded up to around 1 km a year.

*Ridges in its surface show how the Lambert Glacier is stressed as it flows down through the Prince Charles Mountains.*

## Ridges and crevasses

The flow rate of a glacier varies in all three dimensions, vertically through its mass, across its path and along its length. This means that the ice is constantly being stretched and compressed. Where it is stretched by flowing over a ridge in its bed, or as it speeds up downstream, it cracks open to form crevasses. Where it is compressed by the sides of a valley or is forced to flow round a mountain in its path, it forms ridges. Glaciers also flow faster in the centre than at the edges of their stream. So complex patterns of crevasses are created, varying from a few millimetres to 30 metres wide, up to 40 metres deep and sometimes several kilometres long.

Although the ice sheet is continually flowing out towards the edges, it is also being replenished by snowfall. Glaciologists are trying to determine whether these two processes are in balance, or whether the ice sheet is growing or decaying. These studies may eventually help to solve the riddle of the Greenhouse effect (☞ pp.104–105).

*Crevasses are the stretch marks of the ice sheet or glacier, running across the direction of flow.*

# Sea ice and icebergs

THE ice-covered continent of Antarctica is itself surrounded by an ice-covered sea for most of the year, which more than doubles the area of Antarctic ice in the winter.

## Sea ice

The sea ice reaches its maximum extent in September, when it covers 20 million $km^2$ of the Southern Ocean and recedes to a minimum of 4 million $km^2$ at the end of February. Freezing is most rapid in May and June when the ice edge advances northwards by as much as 4 km a day. As it spreads the ice also thickens, by the freezing of water underneath and the addition of snow on top. By midwinter it can reach a thickness of 3–4 metres and form floes many kilometres across.

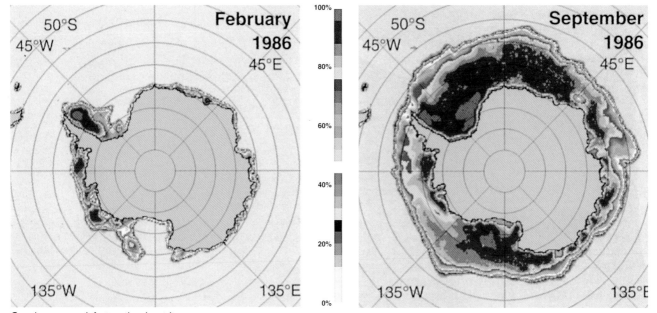

Sea ice around Antarctica is at its minimum at the end of February (above), when only the Weddell Sea retains any great amount. By September, the ice cover has increased fivefold and is at its maximum (right). The coloured scale shows the density of the ice cover, as measured in these satellite images.

The sea ice varies in density (see the diagram above). Within the total area there may be as much as 20% open water in pools known as polynyas, and in channels between floes. The ice is constantly moving because of storms and ocean currents. Floes can be rafted up on top of each other, or forced edge to edge in pressure ridges, making it very dangerous for ships.

## Sea ice and climate

The formation of sea ice has a major effect on Antarctica's climate, though the relationship between them is not yet well understood. Like the continental ice sheet, sea ice reflects most of the sun's energy back into the atmosphere. So its presence in spring delays the warming effect of the returning sun and its re-formation in autumn hastens the cooling of the continent. It also makes the air much drier by preventing the exchange of water vapour between the ocean and the atmosphere. This is one reason why so little moisture reaches the continent, and so little snow falls in the centre. On a broader scale, changes in sea ice influence ocean and weather conditions, and these in turn affect the distribution of sea ice. The amount of sea ice varies greatly from year to year and area to area as a result.

## Sea ice and ocean circulation

Sea ice is formed in autumn and winter by the freezing of fairly pure water, so the surface water left behind is much saltier than the layers below. It is also much colder, and both these factors make it heavier, so it sinks. In spring and summer, thawing of the ice produces the opposite effect, creating a layer of lighter, less salty water on the surface of the ocean. Both these processes have a major impact on the circulation of currents in the Southern Ocean, and on its marine life (☛ pp. 54–55).

## Icebergs

As well as sea ice which comes and goes in a seasonal cycle, the Southern Ocean around Antarctica is invaded annually by thousands of icebergs. One survey in 1985 found 30 000 icebergs in an area of about 4000 km$^2$. They are not formed by freezing of the sea, but come from the outward flow of the continental ice sheet (☛ p. 24). Some are formed by the collapse of ice cliffs or a glacier tongue flowing directly into the sea. About 80% are calved from the ice shelves into which major glaciers flow. These 'tabular' icebergs are also the largest, like the monster chunk of the Ross Ice Shelf covering 31 000 km$^2$ which broke off in 1956.

## Iceberg voyages

Once released, icebergs are carried northward and westward at up to 8 km a day in the easterly wind and currents around the continent until they reach the Antarctic Convergence (☛ p. 8). There they meet warmer water and they rapidly melt. The furthest north an iceberg has been sighted was at 26°30′S in the South Atlantic, almost in the tropics!

Most icebergs take several seasons over this process, and some are grounded for years in shallow bays where they become part of the local scenery. Overall, about 2 million tonnes of the Antarctic ice sheet is calved off each year in icebergs. This is equivalent to nearly half the world's drinking water. It has been suggested that icebergs could be towed to dry countries like Australia and melted to supply water, but the technical problems are enormous.

*When the sea starts to freeze, it forms thin plates of ice which are jostled together by wind and wave action into pancakes, like white water lilies.*

*Pancakes soon freeze together and thicken, adding ice below and snow on top to form ice floes which in turn make up pack ice.*

*A crack like this (above) across an ice shelf will eventually calve a tabular iceberg (left), which is starting its voyage to warmer waters.*

## Dispelling the myths

ANTARCTICA remained remote, undiscovered and shrouded in mystery long after human migration had settled the other six continents. It was *Terra Australis Incognita*, an unknown south land, as the map below illustrates.

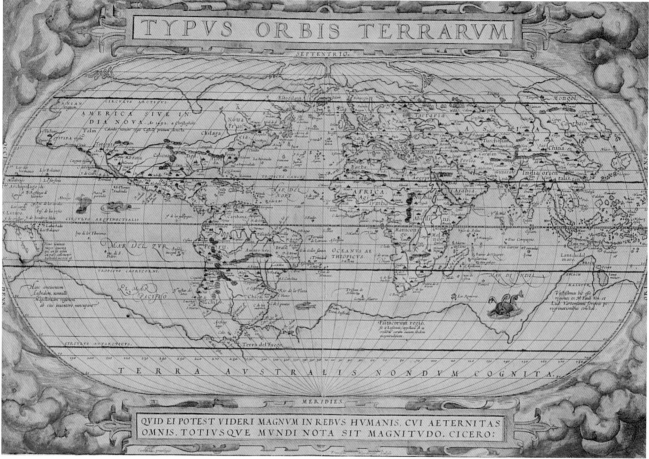

*This map of the world drawn in 1570 shows 'Terra Australis Nondum Cognita' — the unknown south land — extending right around the globe. It incorporates Australia and is attached to the tip of South America.*

The existence of this great south land was derived from the ideas of the early Greek geographers. They believed there must be a large landmass around the South Pole to 'balance' the known land in the northern hemisphere. They named it the opposite of the Arctic, the *Anti-Arktikos* or Antarctic. The discoveries of Sir Francis Drake (1577–80) and Abel Tasman (1642–44) severed first South America and then Australia from this huge imagined southern continent. Even so, 300 years ago Antarctica was still thought to cover almost all the globe south of 50° South — nearly five times its actual size. So the discovery of Antarctica was a process of discovering where it wasn't, rather than where it was.

### Captain James Cook

The great navigator Captain James Cook was the first to tackle this puzzle. In three summers' exploration between 1772 and 1775, he crossed the Antarctic Circle (66°30′S) four times and reached 71°10′S, so dispelling the myth of *Terra Australis Incognita*. Cook discovered no land, and he claimed 'that no man will ever venture farther than I have done, and that the lands which may lie to the south will never be explored'.

## Sealers explore the Antarctic Peninsula

However, what Cook did find was a wealth of marine life. To exploit this, sealers became the most active Antarctic explorers for the next century.

The bonanza started in 1819, when William Smith was blown south across Drake Passage in a gale and accidentally discovered the South Shetland Islands. At least 30 American and 25 British sealing ships visited the islands the next summer. One harvested 14 000 skins in five weeks. Soon the sealers were searching further afield. In 1820 Nathaniel Palmer discovered the islands along the coast of the Antarctic Peninsula, and John Davis reached the Peninsula itself and made the first recorded landing on the continent. In 1822 James Weddell found a huge ice-free sea east of the Peninsula reaching to 74°15′S, well beyond Cook's most southerly latitude.

## Russian interest

Meanwhile the Russians were expanding their interest from the north to the south polar regions. In 1819 Admiral Thaddeus von Bellingshausen led an expedition to follow up some of Cook's discoveries. His two-year circumnavigation solved several additional pieces of the puzzle and narrowed the boundaries of the continent still more.

In 1830 an English sealing company, Enderby Brothers, was looking for yet more new sealing grounds. So they ordered their captain, John Biscoe, to take two ships and head south east from the Falkland Islands. Over the next two seasons Biscoe circumnavigated Antarctica, and in February 1831 he sighted the mountains of Enderby Land in East Antarctica. With this discovery, Biscoe proved that Antarctica did indeed contain a large land mass, and challenged Cook's claim that it could never be explored.

## Voyages to Antarctica 1770–1830

**1772–75** ——— first – – – second ······· third ▶
**James Cook** (Britain)
*Resolution* and *Adventure*

**1819** ————▶
**William Smith** (Britain)
*Williams*

**1819–20** ———▷
**Edward Bransfield** (Britain)
*Williams*

**1819–21** ————▶
**Thaddeus von Bellingshausen** (Russia )
*Vostok* and *Mirnyi*

**1820–21** ————▶
**Nathaniel Palmer** (United States)
*Hero*

**1820–21** ———▷
**John Davis** (United States)
*Cecilia*

**1822–24** ————▶
**James Weddell** (Britain)
*Jane* and *Beaufoy*

**1830–32** ————▶
**John Biscoe** (Britain)
*Tula* and *Lively*

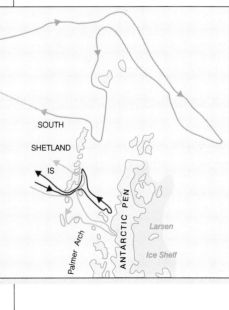

## The international assault

*So eager was Borchgrevink to be first ashore on the continent he leapt from the boat into the freezing water.*

A T FIRST, the British and the Americans were the most active in exploring Antarctica, to exploit seals for commercial gain. But soon other nations began to follow the lead of the Russians in scientific exploration. In the 25 years after Bellingshausen returned, three major national expeditions were sent out by France, Britain and the United States.

### Scientific curiosity

One puzzle they tried to solve was the exact position of the South Magnetic Pole. This would enable scientists to understand more about the earth's magnetic core, and help make more accurate compasses. Both d'Urville and Ross tried to locate it without success. However, in searching for the Magnetic Pole, Ross discovered the huge ice shelf at the head of the Ross Sea, which provided the easiest access to the South Pole for later explorers.

### National claims

The mid 19th century was a period when many European nations were seeking new colonies. At the same time, sealing was making Antarctica commercially important. So both the French and the British were keen to acquire territory in Antarctica. To achieve this, an expedition had to find some land, fix its position, raise the flag, claim it for their ruler, and get back home to tell everyone. But it is hard to tell real 'land' from floating ice shelves or icebergs, and many claims were disputed or disproved. For example, Wilkes, the leader of the United States Exploring Expedition, claimed to have seen 'land' which other ships later sailed over (☞ p. 38).

In fact these land claims had little value compared to new colonies in Africa or Asia, so after the initial enthusiasm, interest in Antarctica faded.

*Borchgrevink's winter base at Cape Adare in 1898 was the first on the continent. He was also the first to use dogs for sledge journeys on the ice.*

## An important discovery

In the next 50 years only the *Challenger* expedition sailed south of the Antarctic Circle. She was the first steam ship to do so, and she made a very important discovery. The further south she went, the more rocks like granite, quartz and limestone she dredged up from the seabed. These are continental rocks, so this could only mean one thing. They must have been carried there embedded in icebergs which melted and dropped them to the seabed. Antarctica, where they came from, must therefore be a continent, not a group of ice-covered islands.

## Renewed interest

In 1895 an International Geographical Congress was held in London to try to revive interest in Antarctic science and exploration. It was so successful that in the next 20 years no fewer than ten nations sent over 20 expeditions to the continent.

As more ships tried to push further into the pack ice to reach the shore, some became trapped and even sunk. *Belgica* was the first to winter in the ice, unintentionally, when she became trapped. Although she escaped unharmed next spring, two crew members went mad as a result. Nordenskjöld's *Antarctic* was not so lucky and was sunk, though her crew were rescued after two desperate winters. Bruce, Drygalski, Charcot, and Filchner were also trapped in their ships.

However Borchgrevink showed that a well planned expedition could winter in comfort on the continent. From Cape Adare he sailed to the Ross Ice Shelf in February 1900 and sledged inland for about 15 km, the furthest south anyone had so far reached.

## Voyages to Antarctica 1830–1912

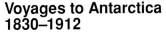

**1837–40** — first ——— second ➤
**Dumont d'Urville** (France)
*Astrolabe* and *Zelee*

**1838–39** ———➤
**John Balleny** (Britain)
*Sabrina* and *Eliza Scott*

**1838–42** — first ——— second ➤
**Charles Wilkes** (United States)
*Vincennes* and others

**1839–43** — first ——— second ➤
**James Clark Ross** (Britain)
*Erebus* and *Terror*

**1872–76** ———➤
**George Nares** (Britain)
*Challenger*

**1897–99** ———➤
**Adrien de Gerlache** (Belgium)
*Belgica*

**1898–1900** ———➤
**Carsten Borchgrevink** (Britain)
*Southern Cross*

**1901–03** ———➤
**Eric von Drygalski** (Germany)
*Gauss*

**1901–03** ———➤
**Otto Nordenskjöld** (Sweden)
*Antarctic*

**1902–04** ———➤
**William Bruce** (Scotland)
*Scotia*

**1903–10** — first ——— second ➤
**Jean Charcot** (France)
*Francais* and *Pourquoi Pas?*

**1911–12** ———➤
**Wilhelm Filchner** (Germany)
*Deutschland*

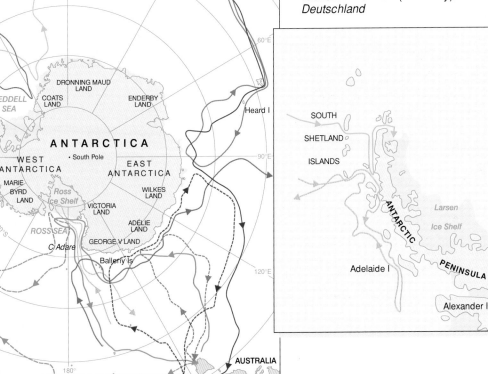

# The race for the South Pole, 1901–09

**W**HILE other nations sent expeditions all around Antarctica after the 1895 International Geographical Congress, the British had only one aim — to be first at the South Pole.

This was the personal ambition of the President of the Royal Geographical Society, Sir Clements Markham. He persuaded his Society to sponsor an expedition, and both the king and the navy to support it. A specially ice-strengthened ship, *Discovery*, was built and Robert Falcon Scott was chosen to command her.

*Captain Robert Falcon Scott, 1868–1912*

## Polar Expeditions 1901–09

1901–04  ⟶
**Robert Scott** (Britain)
*Discovery*

1907–09  ⟶
**Ernest Shackleton** (Britain)
*Nimrod*

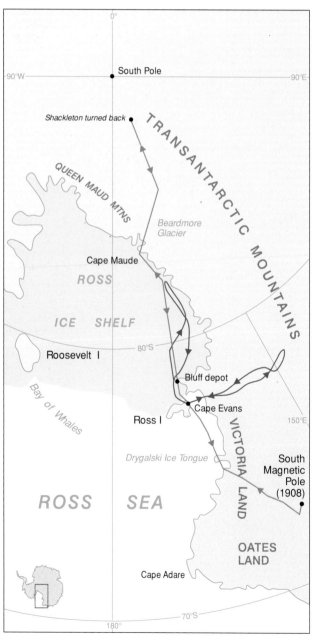

## Scott's *Discovery* expedition

Scott reached the Ross Sea, the gateway to the Pole, in January 1902. He sailed east along the Ross Ice Shelf but could find nowhere to land. The ice cliffs formed a frustrating barrier up to 80 metres high. At the Bay of Whales Scott went up in a tethered balloon — the first flight in Antarctica — to try and see what lay beyond. The ice shelf stretched like a level highway to the south, if only he could get onto it. Eventually he found a good anchorage for *Discovery* off Ross Island, where he spent the winter on board, carrying out scientific research.

Next spring Scott prepared his attack on the Pole, laying depots of food and fuel to the south. Then on 2 November with Edward Wilson and Ernest Shackleton as companions and 19 dogs pulling five sledges, he set off with high hopes. But things soon began to go wrong. None of the men were experienced drivers, and the dogs refused to pull. Even worse, one by one they died. Snow blindness, hunger and frostbite weakened the explorers. By 30 December, having reached 82°16′S, they had had enough. Without fresh food, scurvy crippled them further as they struggled back to the ship.

All three men took time to recover, but Scott was convinced that Shackleton had 'broken down' on the return journey and sent him home on the relief ship. This was an insult Shackleton never forgave, and the former companions became rivals.

## Shackleton's *Nimrod* expedition

Shackleton was determined to make his own bid for the Pole, and by 1907 he had managed to raise enough money to buy food, equipment and an old sealing ship, the *Nimrod*. Disappointed by the dogs' performance on Scott's expedition, Shackleton decided to try Siberian ponies instead. He also took the first car to Antarctica (☞ p. 73), though it soon broke down in the cold.

In January 1908 when Shackleton reached the Ross Sea he turned east. This was partly because a winter base in this area would mean the least distance to the Pole. In addition, Scott had claimed the Ross Island region as 'his' territory, and Shackleton had agreed to avoid it. But pack ice barred his way and the Bay of Whales had disappeared in a massive breakout of the ice shelf (☞ p. 27). Now there was nowhere else *except* Ross Island for a winter base. So despite his promise to his rival Shackleton was forced to return there .

*Sir Ernest Shackleton, 1874–1922*

*Shackleton and his two companions at their furthest south point.*

Next spring, one party which included Douglas Mawson set out to locate the South Magnetic Pole in Victoria Land (☞ p. 30). Shackleton with three companions and the four remaining ponies pulling the sledges, headed for the main goal. They soon passed Scott's furthest south point. At the end of the ice shelf they found a natural staircase, the Beardmore Glacier. This took them through the Transantarctic Mountains and up onto the polar plateau. It was a steep and dangerous climb, criss-crossed by crevasses. The last pony fell into one and could not be rescued. On the plateau, at over 3000 metres, it was far colder and windier and the thinner air made manhauling the sledge harder than ever.

## Shackleton turns back

By 9 January, Shackleton had to face an agonising choice. They were at 88°23′S, only 160 km from the Pole. With the food they had left, they could reach the Pole, or they could get back to base; but not both. As Shackleton later wrote to his wife 'I would rather be a live donkey than a dead lion' and so they turned back. On his return to England, Shackleton was showered with praise for his achievement. But this only increased Scott's determination to outdo his rival.

# The race for the South Pole, 1910–13

DESPITE Shackleton's achievement Sir Clements Markham, the President of the Royal Geographical Society, still wanted an Englishman to be first at the South Pole. So he helped Scott organise another expedition.

## Scott's second expedition

Scott's second expedition reached Ross Island in the *Terra Nova* in January 1911. Next spring he set out from his base at Cape Evans for the Pole once more. This time, although he took both ponies and dogs, Scott intended to rely on manhauling for most of the journey. He followed Shackleton's track to the top of the Beardmore Glacier. On the plateau, the last of the support parties turned back, leaving Scott and his four companions, Evans, Oates, Bowers and Wilson, with 240 km to go.

## Struggle for survival

They reached their goal on 17 January 1912, but their joy and relief were overwhelmed by disappointment. Amundsen had beaten them to it by over a month. Now, as well as hunger, cold and illness they carried the burden of failure in their desperate struggle for survival. Evans was the first to die, after a fall into a crevasse. A month later Oates's feet were so painfully frostbitten that he was delaying the whole party. Tormented by this knowledge he left the tent one night in a blizzard with the words 'I am just going outside and I may be some time'. He was never seen again.

The three survivors stumbled on. It was now late March and winter was fast approaching. When a blizzard pinned them in their tent for a week without food, only 18 km from their next depot, it was the end. Their bodies were found next spring by a search party. Scott's diary was open beside him, the last entry dated 29 March. So who was the intruder who snatched the great prize from the British?

## Polar Expeditions 1910–13

**1910–12** *by sledge* →
**Roald Amundsen** (Norway)
*Fram*

**1910–13** *by sledge* → *by ship* →
**Robert Scott** (Britain)
*Terra Nova*

*Amundsen, Hanssen, Hassel and Wistig just before leaving the South Pole on 17 December 1911. 'Farewell dear Pole, I don't think we'll meet again' said Amundsen.*

*Oates, Bowers, Scott, Wilson and Evans (from left) at the South Pole on 18 January 1912. 'Great God, this is an awful place' said Scott.*

## Amundsen

Roald Amundsen was a Norwegian with years of Arctic exploration behind him. He had also wintered in Antarctica on the *Belgica* in 1898 (☛ p. 31). His original goal was the North Pole. But that was conquered in 1909, just when Amundsen had got his expedition organised. So he switched his sights to the South. Only weeks after Scott arrived at Ross Island, Amundsen reached the Bay of Whales. From there, he had 100 km less to travel to the Pole than Scott.

## Amundsen used dogs

In addition he had 97 dogs, and years of experience in the Norwegian tradition of dog driving on skis. These skills gave him a huge advantage over Scott. With four companions and four sledges pulled by 13 dogs each, Amundsen set off for the Pole on 20 October 1911.

*Roald Amundsen, 1872–1928*

This was only four days before Scott, but he was able to travel much faster. He averaged 25–30 km a day compared to Scott's 15–20 km. Also, because the Transantarctic Mountains run south east (☛ map), more of Amundsen's route was on the ice shelf and less was on the higher, colder plateau than Scott's. But Amundsen was pioneering a new route. He was confronted by an even steeper glacier with huge ice falls as his only way through the mountains.

## Amundsen's triumph

Once on the plateau, the route was much easier, and by 14 December 1911 his party reached the Pole. After spending three days there to fix their position accurately, they set off for home, now with only eleven dogs. The rest had been killed in stages to feed the remainder. This careful planning and the laying of frequent depots gave Amundsen a reliable lifeline on the return journey, unlike Scott.

Once back at the Bay of Whales the expedition was picked up by the *Fram*, and on 7 March 1912 Amundsen cabled the news of his triumph to the world — from the Hobart Post Office.

# The Imperial Transantarctic Expedition

Endurance *trapped in the ice of the Weddell Sea, photographed by moonlight.*

**A**LTHOUGH Scott became a national hero after his death became known in 1913, it was still a blow to British pride that the great prize had gone to another country.

Shackleton's reputation was still high, and with the Pole conquered by others, his restless spirit and love of Antarctica had to find a new challenge. So when he chose the most ambitious challenge of all — to cross the continent from the Weddell to the Ross Sea via the Pole — it was greeted with enthusiastic support. It would need two ships and two expeditions. One to land the party at Vahsel Bay in Coats Land for the crossing; the other to winter at Ross Island and lay depots to the south to provide supplies for the last leg of the journey.

## The voyage south

After a year of preparation, Shackleton was ready to sail in August 1914, just as World War I broke out in Europe. He offered his ship and men to the war effort, but the British government decided that the expedition was of greater value to national morale.

So Shackleton sailed south once more. His ship *Endurance* had been built specially for the voyage. He left South Georgia in December, and made good progress towards Vahsel Bay by dodging through the pack ice. He was lucky to find an ice-free channel along the coast. But then the wind changed and closed the channel. Shackleton tried desperately to find a way out but it was no use. On 18 January 1915 *Endurance* became firmly locked into the ice.

## *Endurance* sinks

For the next ten months she drifted north west. Gradually the ice pressed closer until *Endurance* finally sank in late November. By then the men had moved all their supplies and the ship's lifeboats to a camp on the ice. With the help of their dogs they hauled everything over the pressure ridges to a safe floe. There they set up 'Patience Camp' and drifted for another five months. Finally, in April 1916 the ice at last set them free. They launched the lifeboats and sailed to the nearest land, Elephant Island off the Antarctic Peninsula.

## Voyage to South Georgia

Launching James Caird *at Elephant Island, on the perilous voyage to South Georgia.*

Leaving most of his men there, Shackleton and four others set out in one of the lifeboats, the *James Caird*. It was 1300 km across one of the world's stormiest oceans to South Georgia, the nearest inhabited island. But they could only land on the south coast, while the whaling station was on the north coast. Shackleton and two others made a final desperate dash to reach help. They had to climb an unknown 1000 metre mountain range, and guess which was the right valley on the other side. Their luck held and they reached the whaling station safely.

## Rescue from Elephant Island

The men left on Elephant Island lived on seals and seaweed. They were afraid they might have to spend the rest of their lives there if Shackleton failed to get through. But on 30 August, three months after they had landed, 'the Boss' brought a ship to their rescue. This is still the greatest Antarctic epic of all, and miraculously not a single life was lost.

Men and dogs of the Ross Sea party landing from Aurora at Cape Evans.

## The Ross Sea saga

Meanwhile, on the other side of the continent another saga was unfolding. The Ross Sea party had the job of laying depots south towards the Pole, to provide food and fuel for Shackleton's party on the last leg of their journey as they crossed from the Weddell Sea.

They landed at Cape Evans in January 1915 and moored their ship *Aurora* to the ice for the winter. But she was blown away in a ferocious blizzard in May, with her crew, and also with most of the stores and fuel still on board. Luckily they found food and equipment left behind by previous expeditions. With this, and the meat and blubber from seals, they lived on for two winters. They even managed to lay all the depots Shackleton had asked for, though they didn't know their efforts were in vain.

Like the men on Elephant Island, they had to live with the fear that *Aurora* had been lost, and so no one knew where they were. But *Aurora* was luckier than *Endurance*. Although she too was trapped in the ice for ten months, she eventually reached New Zealand intact. There she was refitted and sent south again in December 1916 on a rescue mission. Shackleton had by then returned from South Georgia and accompanied the ship. So it was with amazement that the Ross Sea party saw their leader approaching over the sea ice from the north, instead of across the ice shelf from the south.

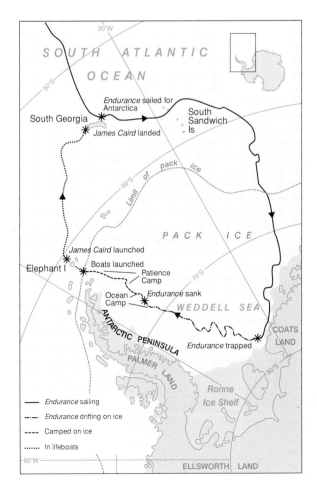

# Sir Douglas Mawson and Australian Antarctica

*Sir Douglas Mawson, 1882–1958*

**M**AWSON first went to Antarctica as the physicist on Shackleton's 1907–09 *Nimrod* expedition. Scott invited him to join his second expedition, but it was Mawson's ambition to lead his own.

As a scientist he was more interested in investigating a new region, rather than pushing the extra 100 km to the South Pole. He wanted to explore the unknown coast of Antarctica directly south of Australia, west of Cape Adare, and in 1910 he organised an expedition to do so.

## Planning the expedition

Combined with his scientific qualifications, Mawson was an outstanding leader and organiser. His plan was to establish four main bases, one at Macquarie Island and three others on the continent. The Macquarie Island base would send regular weather observations to Melbourne by radio. For the first time in Antarctica, both the Main Base and the expedition ship *Aurora* had radio as well. Mawson also planned to use an aircraft, another Antarctic first. However, it was damaged in Australia, and so only the fuselage and engine were taken, and used as an 'air tractor' (☛ p. 73).

## Aurora's voyage

After leaving Hobart, *Aurora* landed the Macquarie Island party then sailed south. She soon met impenetrable pack ice, and turned southwestwards, looking for land. Mawson eventually found an ice-free bay and a rocky cape on which to set up his Main Base. From Commonwealth Bay, Captain John Davis pushed *Aurora* westwards looking for the land recorded by Wilkes in 1840, the last to have sailed this coast (☛ p. 31). But after nearly a month and 3000 km he could find none. So he was finally forced to leave the Western party, not on solid land but on the Shackleton Ice Shelf.

*Aurora made three voyages to Antarctica. She carried out the biggest research program in Antarctic waters since the Challenger expedition (☛ p. 31).*

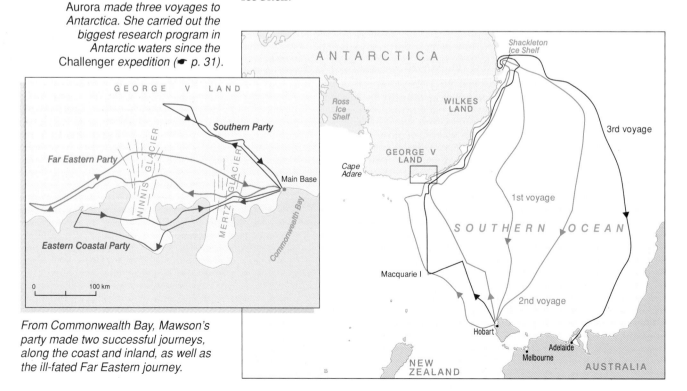

*From Commonwealth Bay, Mawson's party made two successful journeys, along the coast and inland, as well as the ill-fated Far Eastern journey.*

## 'The Home of the Blizzard'

Back at Main Base Mawson's party were discovering that they had chosen 'the Home of the Blizzard' for their winter quarters. The katabatic wind (☛ p. 20) roared down from the ice sheet rising steeply behind them, gusting to 200 km/h. Merely living in such conditions was a battle for survival; travelling inland was even worse.

## Disaster strikes

Mawson had chosen dogs as his main form of transport, and hired two expert drivers, Ninnis and Mertz. Next spring these three men and the twelve best dogs made up the Far Eastern exploring party (☛map). Despite the cold and wind they made good progress until disaster struck. On 14 December 1912, Ninnis, with his sledge carrying the tent and most of the food, and the six fittest dogs, disappeared down a crevasse.

Mawson and Mertz were left 500 km from base, with barely any food and no tent. They killed and ate their remaining dogs, finding the livers easiest to chew. Then Mertz became ill and too weak to march, and died after a sudden fit, probably of Vitamin A poisoning from the dog livers.

## Struggle for survival

Now Mawson was alone, still 160 km from base, and desperately ill himself. Cutting his sledge in half to save weight, he stumbled on. Only 50 km from base he found a food dump which saved his life. It had been left by a search party and he had missed them by only two hours. But an even more dramatic near miss was in store. Delayed by blizzards Mawson finally reached Main Base five days later, just in time to see *Aurora* disappearing to the north. She was urgently recalled by radio but the ferocious winds prevented her from returning. Davis could not wait. He had to rescue the Western base party, who had no supplies for a second winter.

The following summer, *Aurora* returned to Commonwealth Bay to retrieve the remaining men. By then Mawson was fully recovered from his ordeal.

*The 40-year-old sealing ship* Aurora *proved more than a match for the appalling weather and endless pack ice, in the skilled hands of Captain John Davis.*

*Mawson's half sledge, which saved his life several times by wedging in the top of a crevasse when he fell through on his hauling rope.*

*This famous shot by Frank Hurley graphically illustrates the endless battle against the wind at Commonwealth Bay.*

## Filling the void

B Y THE end of the first phase of Antarctic exploration in 1917, less than 5% of the continent had actually been surveyed. When interest in Antarctica revived a decade later, new techniques of aerial photography rapidly expanded the rate of surveying and mapping.

### First Antarctic flight

In 1928 Sir Hubert Wilkins made the first Antarctic flight across 1000 km of the Peninsula, equipped with a hand-held camera. The following year an American expedition led by Richard Byrd made an aerial survey of Amundsen's route ( p. 34). He flew from the Bay of Whales on the Ross Sea to the Pole and back in 16 hours. Amundsen had taken three months.

In East Antarctica, Sir Douglas Mawson led two expeditions in 1929–31. They surveyed the coast from Cape Adare to Enderby Land, to reinforce the British claim to what is now the Australian Antarctic Territory ( maps pp. 6, 87). He used a Gipsy Moth seaplane to make aerial photo-

In 1925, only about 5% of Antarctica had been explored.

In 1950, most of the coastline was known.

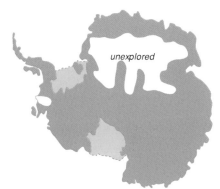

In 1959, only a small area was still a blank on the map.

graphs and sketch maps. At the same time a Norwegian expedition surveyed the coast further west. By 1940 much of the coast of East Antarctica had been sighted and named, but very few landings had actually been made.

### Large scale mapping

The modern period of Antarctic exploration began after World War II. In 1946, the United States set the future pattern with Operation Highjump. It was a large expedition consisting of 13 ships, 23 aircraft and over 4000 men in three separate task forces. Its objective was to photograph the entire Antarctic coastline. Altogether, Operation Highjump took over 70 000 aerial photographs of nearly 4 million km$^2$ of Antarctica, covering about 60% of the coast and interior; 25% had never been seen before.

But aerial photographs are not maps. They have to be related to known features. So the following year surveyors were landed by helicopter on peaks and rocks shown in the photographs, to fix their position and height.

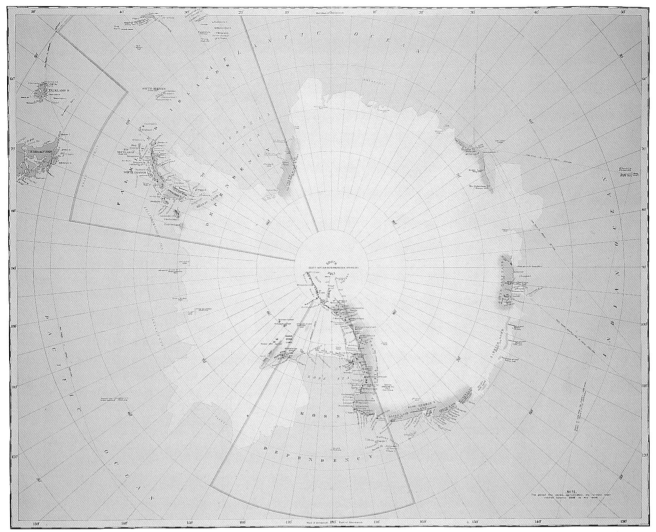

*The first Australian map of Antarctica, published in 1929, detailed only fragments of the coast. Compare it with the present day map on p. 6.*

By 1950, although almost the entire coastline was known, the interior of East Antarctica remained a blank on the map. In the next decade land traverses by dog teams, snowmobiles and tractors gnawed away at this void. The International Geophysical Year of 1957–58 (☛ p. 95) increased this activity and saw the first crossing of the continent from the Weddell to the Ross Sea.

## Satellite technology

Antarctic mapping has been revolutionalised in the last 20 years by two major advances in satellite technology. The first was the development of remote sensing. From the 1970s this made satellite images of Antarctica available. One image could show the area covered by a thousand aerial photographs and also reveal areas that had never been photographed. The second more recent advance is GPS, or the Global Positioning System. These computerised instruments can receive signals from satellites moving in known orbits around the earth. By measuring the distance from four or more satellites at the same time, the computer can work out its exact position and height on the ground. One GPS fix of a key point on a map can be used to recalculate the heights and locations of other features measured by earlier methods.

With these two technologies increasingly accurate maps of Antarctica can be produced, like the one on the cover of this book, which finally dispel the myth of *Terra Australis Incognita*.

# Human settlement in Antarctica

Greenpeace base at Cape Evans on Ross Island.

T HE earliest settlers in the Antarctic were the sealers. From the early 19th century they built primitive shelters on the offshore islands. Carsten Borchgrevink set up the first base on the continent, at Cape Adare in 1899 (☛ p. 30). The oldest continuously occupied settlement is the Argentine base of Orcadas in the South Orkney Islands. It was originally built as a meteorological station in 1903. Scott set up his first winter base at Hut Point on Ross Island in 1901. This and two other huts built by Shackleton in 1907 and Scott in 1911 (☛ pp. 32–34) are still standing.

Amundsen built his base on the Ross Ice Shelf at the Bay of Whales, but it has never been seen since he left it in 1912. That piece of the ice shelf probably broke away as an iceberg, carrying the base with it. Mawson's hut is still standing at Commonwealth Bay (☛ p. 39). It badly needs restoration but the ferocious climate makes this very difficult.

## Permanent bases

Permanent bases were not set up until after World War II when a new period of scientific research and exploration began. Australia was a leader in this new phase and in 1954 set up the first permanent base on the continent. This was at Mawson on the coast of East Antarctica (☛ p. 84). Soon after, the International Geophysical Year in 1957–58 (☛ p. 94) created a surge of interest in Antarctic research, and 50 stations were established by twelve nations. As part of this program, the United States built the first permanent inland station, Amundsen–Scott, at the South Pole in 1957, while the USSR established Vostok the following year.

One major problem for permanent settlements in Antarctica is finding a suitable spot for a station, because only 2% of the continent is ice-free

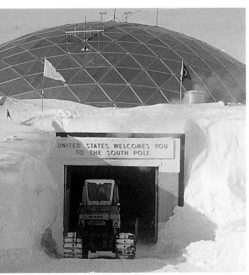

Amundsen–Scott station at the South Pole is the world's most inaccessible human settlement.

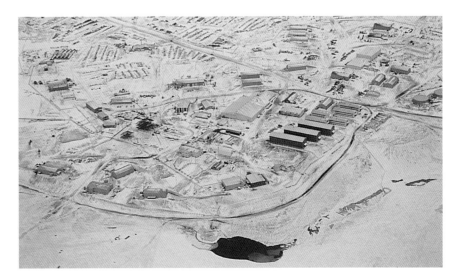

The US McMurdo station on Ross Island is now a small town.

(☞ p. 14). Stations built on ice tend to sink under their own weight as the heat they generate melts the surrounding ice. Others can get buried in snow.

## Private expeditions

As well as the big government funded stations, some private expeditions have set up smaller bases in recent years. Greenpeace, the international environmental organisation, maintained a base on Ross Island for five years from 1987, as part of its campaign to conserve Antarctica (☞ p. 92). Other private expeditions come by yacht, and one froze theirs into the ice for the winter, like some of the early explorers (☞ pp. 30–31).

## Population of Antarctica

There are now 37 permanent Antarctic bases run by 17 nations, with another four on subantarctic islands. The greatest concentration is along the Antarctic Peninsula, and there are eight on King George Island alone. As well, up to 30 field camps operate each year during the summer months.

The population of Antarctica in winter is about 1000 people, rising to around 4000 in summer. This will grow even more as tourism increases (☞ p. 96). Australia's three stations contribute about one-tenth of this total. The largest station is the US base at McMurdo on Ross Island, with about 300 people in winter and 1200 in summer. Antarctic 'settlers' are now mostly scientists, technicians and maintenance workers, and the gender ratio is around 10:1 in favour of males. With only one person per 14 000 km$^2$, human settlement in Antarctica is far sparser than anywhere else, but it is now a permanent feature of the continent.

| OPERATING STATIONS IN ANTARCTICA Winter 1992 | |
|---|---|
| ARGENTINA | Belgrano II |
| | Esperanza |
| | Jubany |
| | Marambio |
| | Orcadas |
| | San Martin |
| AUSTRALIA | Casey |
| | Davis |
| | Mawson |
| BRAZIL | Commandante Ferraz |
| CHILE | Capitan Arturo Prat |
| | General Bernado O'Higgins |
| | Teniente Rodolfo Marsh |
| FRANCE | Dumont d'Urville |
| GERMANY | Georg von Neumayer |
| INDIA | Maitri |
| JAPAN | Asuka |
| | Syowa |
| NEW ZEALAND | Scott Base |
| PEOPLE'S REP. OF CHINA | Great Wall |
| | Zhongshan |
| POLAND | Arctowski |
| REP. OF KOREA | King Sejong |
| RUSSIA | Bellingshausen |
| | Mirny |
| | Molodezhnaya |
| | Novolazarevskaya |
| | Vostok |
| SOUTH AFRICA | SANAE |
| UK | Faraday |
| | Halley |
| | Rothera |
| | Signy |
| URUGUAY | Artigas |
| USA | Amundsen-Scott |
| | McMurdo |
| | Palmer |

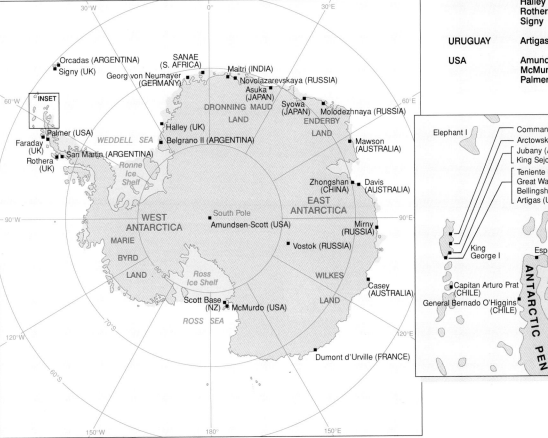

## Images of Antarctica

This poster advertising Frank Hurley's film of Shackleton's Endurance expedition sums up the image of the heroic age.

**A**NTARCTICA is a continent of the imagination. It has inspired artists to create poetry, drama, painting and photography that captures its impact on the human spirit. Some of these words and images are represented here.

*Gustave Dore illustrated Samuel Taylor Coleridge's The Rime of the Ancient Mariner, the first poem about Antarctica.*

With sloping masts and dipping prow,
As who pursued with yell and blow
Still treads the shadow of his foe,
And forward bends his head,
The ship drove fast, loud roared the blast,
And southward aye we fled.

And now there came both mist and snow,
And it grew wondrous cold:
And ice, mast-high, came floating by,
As green as emerald.

And through the drifts the snowy clifts
Did send a dismal sheen:
Nor shapes of men nor beasts we ken —
The ice was all between.

The ice was here, the ice was there,
The ice was all around:
It cracked and growled, and roared and howled,
Like noises in a swound !

At length did cross an Albatross,
Thorough the fog it came:
As if it had been a Christian soul,
We hailed it in God's name.

It ate the food it ne'er had eat,
And round and round it flew.
The ice did split with a thunder-fit;
The helmsman steered us through!

Sidney Nolan depicts the grandeur of the Antarctic landscape.

Mount Erebus on Ross Island dominated the winter bases of Scott's and Shackleton's expedition. It inspired this watercolour by Edward Wilson, and a poem by Shackleton.

Keeper of the Southern Gateway,
    grim, rugged, gloomy and grand;
Warden of these wastes uncharted,
    as the years sweep on, you stand.
At your head the swinging smoke-cloud;
    at your feet the grinding floes;
Racked and seared by the inner fires,
    gripped close by the outer snows.
Proud, unconquered, and unyielding,
    whilst the untold aeons passed,
Inviolate through the ages,
    your ramparts spurning the blast,
Till men impelled by a strong desire,
    broke through your icy bars;
Fierce was the fight to gain that height
    where your stern peak dares the stars.

Jan Senbergs's image of Mawson station shows a jumble of buildings perched precariously on the edge of the vast ice sheet.

Herbert Ponting's photograph of the Terra Nova creates a romantic image out of the stark beauty of Antarctica.

# The Antarctic ecosystem: An overview

## LAND

The terrestrial ecosystem is very simple, with few species and small numbers of individuals. There are no vertebrates.

Midge

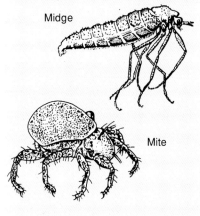

Mite

Collembola

Tardigrade

Nematode

Rotifer

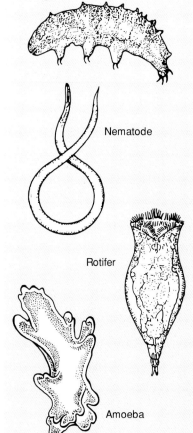

Amoeba

T HE Antarctic ecosystem is made up of a number of separate but interrelated environments with different degrees of species diversity and different levels of productivity.

## Few land species

The terrestrial ecosystem of the Antarctic continent, with only 2% of its area free of ice, is one of the simplest ecosystems on Earth. Wide variations in sunlight and temperature during the year mean that only a few, highly specialised plants and animals can survive there. In addition, the isolation of· the continent means that few new species have been introduced in recent geological time.

Simple plants like lichens and algae are best able to survive in the cold, dry conditions. Amongst the animals, only invertebrates can live year round on the continent. About 200 species have so far been discovered. They range from simple single-celled microscopic protozoans, through rotifers and tardigrades, which are up to 0.5 mm long, to the largest permanent inhabitant, a midge about 10 mm long.

## Lakes are less extreme

Fresh and salt water lakes provide a less extreme environment where a few more species of plankton, algae and mosses can survive. However their growth and productivity is severely restricted by the months of winter darkness, when some lakes freeze solid.

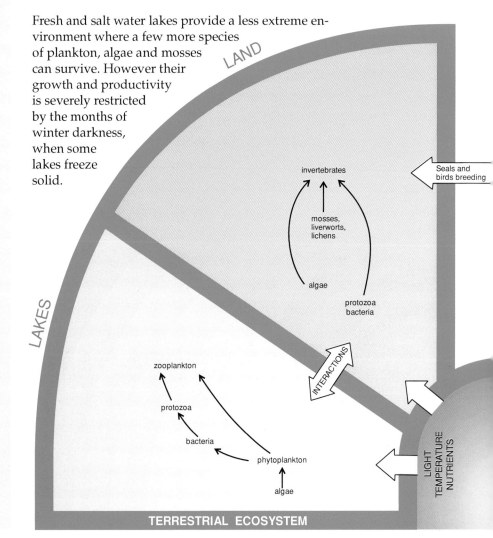

## Subantarctic is more hospitable

The Antarctic Peninsula and nearby islands, and the subantarctic islands which have deeper soils and milder temperatures, support more species of plants and invertebrates. Even so, there are still no higher animals that complete their life cycle on land.

## Many marine species

By comparison the Antarctic marine environment is far richer and more diverse. Water temperatures are more stable than on land, and ocean currents have brought a constant flow of new species, gradually building up an interacting web of plants and animals.

Phytoplankton — tiny plants — are the primary food source, on which thousands of other species depend. These range from zooplankton — tiny animals — to the blue whale, the largest creature that has ever lived. One of the most important elements of this food web (☞ below) is krill — a small crustacean. It feeds on plankton, and in turn is the main food for many species of fish, seals, penguins, sea birds and whales. About 600 000 billion krill (far outweighing the total human population on earth) live in the Southern Ocean.

## Links between land and ocean

Many seals, penguins and other sea birds breed on the shores of the continent and islands, and so link the marine and terrestrial environments together into a single ecosystem.

**OCEAN**

The marine ecosystem is far more complex and diverse, with many thousand species and billions of individuals, for example, krill.

Baleen Whale

Sperm Whale

Seal

Penguins

Seabirds

Squid

Krill

Zooplankton

Fish

Mollusc

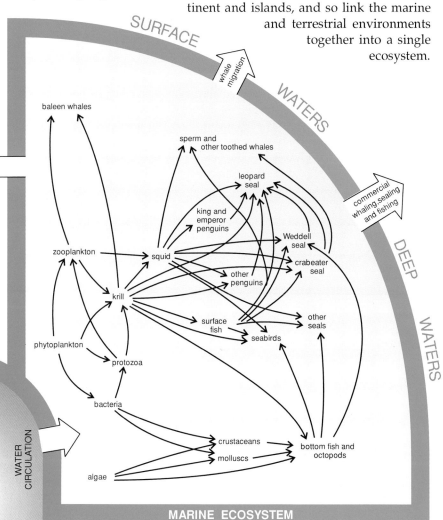

MARINE ECOSYSTEM

# Survival 1: Keeping warm

ALL animals and plants have water in their cells, but in Antarctica almost all water freezes into ice. This can destroy the cells' function and damage the tissues, because water expands when it freezes.

Plants and animals have two kinds of strategies to cope with this. Plants and cold blooded animals, like fish and insects, keep their body fluids around freezing and modify them to avoid cell damage. Warm blooded animals, like mammals and birds, keep their body temperature above freezing, and have ways of preventing heat loss.

## Cold blooded animals

These live mostly in the ocean which is the easiest Antarctic environment to adapt to, as the temperature range is small. Sea water freezes at around –1.8°C and beneath the pack ice remains unfrozen all year. Invertebrates like krill or plankton only freeze if the sea freezes and so they have no problems unless they get trapped in the ice.

Fish are more vulnerable, however, because their body fluids are less concentrated than sea water, and so they freeze at a higher temperature — around –1.1°C. Many Antarctic fish contain 'anti-freeze' molecules in their body fluids, which lower the freezing point to around –2°C and so keep them mobile.

## Ice fish

Even more unusual are the ice fishes, like *Chaenodraco wilsoni*, which have virtually eliminated their red blood cells. Although their blood can carry only 10% as much oxygen as in normal fish, it is much thinner and easier to pump at low temperatures. Their hearts are twice as big and work harder pumping more blood, but overall this takes less energy, especially when the fish is resting.

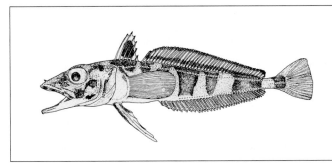

Chaenodraco wilsoni *has no red cells in its blood to make it thinner and easier to pump.*

*The Antarctic fur seal has the thickest coat of any animal.*

## Land animals

Land animals and plants are exposed to a much greater temperature range, from around +15/20°C to –20/30°C, including frequent freeze-thaw cycles. Plants survive these conditions by losing water from their cells to create more concentrated fluids, which freeze at a lower temperature.

In land invertebrates, food in the gut provides a focus for freezing, so most Antarctic insects fast as soon as the temperature begins to fall at the end of summer. Some, like the mite *Alaskozetes antarcticus,* also produce anti-freeze molecules in their body fluids, which enable them to survive at –25°C.

*A male emperor penguin keeps its tiny chick warm in a pouch over its feet.*

## Warm blooded animals

While cold blooded animals adapt their internal environment to the extremes of the external environment, warm blooded animals maintain their internal environment and protect it from external extremes.

Their main strategy is insulation. Whales, seals and penguins all have a thick layer of blubber beneath the skin to maintain their body heat. Seals and penguins overlay this with fur and feathers to increase their resistance to cold. The Antarctic fur seal grows the densest coat of any animal, with an inner layer of very fine hair and an outer, coarser covering.

## Penguins

Emperor penguins, some of which spend all winter on the ice, grow a dense, overlapping coat of feathers with woolly down beneath. The males incubate the eggs on their feet through the long cold winter, huddling together in large groups. The huddle moves constantly across the ice, as birds in the centre are pushed out by others from the edges in a slowly circling whirlpool. It has been calculated that this communal behaviour pattern saves up to 50% of the heat an individual bird would lose each day.

*Emperor penguins huddle together through the winter to conserve body heat while incubating their eggs.*

# Survival 2: Feeding and reproducing

THE two most important factors in the Antarctic ecosystem are temperature and light. To survive and reproduce, an organism must be able to adapt to low temperatures and to eat; and the amount of light determines the food supply.

The extreme variation in sunlight between seasons in the Antarctic causes a large variation in food supply. This means that there is a very short but a very intense growing season for most plants and animals.

## Food supply

The ocean can produce far more food than the limited ice-free land, but during winter the thick covering of pack ice cuts off what little light there is and this reduces the food supply. As the ice forms, algae — microscopic single-celled plants — are trapped in it and lodge on the underside. When spring comes and the ice breaks up, sunlight penetrates again. The effect is dramatic. Within days a 'bloom' of rapidly multiplying algae develops. Each year thousands of millions of tonnes of these and other phytoplankton are produced, providing food for zooplankton and krill. Adults spawn and juveniles mature rapidly throughout the summer, becoming less active as winter approaches once more. All the animals in the marine ecosystem (☛ p. 47) must take maximum advantage of this short-lived food supply.

## Growth rates

Seals and baleen (krill-eating) whales in particular have very rapid growth rates. Blue, fin and sei whales reach about 75% of their maximum length and 40% of their maximum weight in their first year. Calves are large at birth, and a blue whale calf can drink up to 600 litres of milk a day and double its weight in a week.

Seals, like whales, are relatively large at birth. They also have their most rapid growth during their first year, and achieve 50–80% of their maximum length by the end of their second. Elephant seals, for example, weigh

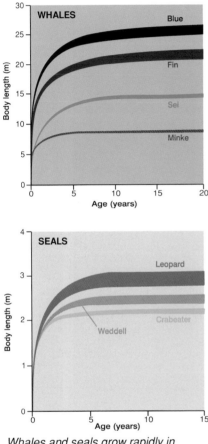

Whales and seals grow rapidly in their first two years.

*Seal pups have a very nutritious food supply on tap.*

up to 50 kg at birth, can double their weight in 14 days, and are weaned, swimming and hunting for themselves, within two months.

## Feeding the young

Young mammals have a food supply immediately available from their mother's milk. Young birds, on the other hand, have to rely on their parents fetching food, often from far away. Most Antarctic seabirds have only 30–50% breeding success because many chicks starve. To increase their chances, all lay large eggs and incubate them for long periods. The chicks when hatched demand 15–20% of their body weight for each meal, which keeps both parents busy. It has been calculated that five million Adélie penguins at one rookery in the South Orkney islands harvest 9000 tonnes of krill a day from the surrounding ocean at the height of the breeding season.

*Penguin chicks must wait longer than seal pups between meals, as their parents have to go further to find food.*

Adélies in turn are a prime target for the major Antarctic predators, the leopard seals and the killer whales, which also need to build up their food reserves to feed their young.

## Land animals

On land, the extreme low temperatures govern growth and survival. Most invertebrates feed only in summer. In winter they prefer to starve rather than freeze (☞ p. 49). Some can lay eggs throughout the summer. Those that do not develop into adults may survive in egg or larval stages to the following summer, and resume their growth in better conditions.

In the harsh Antarctic environment, with great competition for seasonal food supplies, most animals share the same feeding and reproductive strategy. They grow fast in short bursts; they mature late and lay a few large eggs or young with a fairly low survival rate; but they increase their chances of reproducing successfully by living a long time and therefore having many opportunities to breed.

*Killer whales are predators on seals and penguins.*

# Habitats 1: Land, the harshest and sparsest

ANTARCTICA has been through many climate cycles. Some of them were much warmer and moister and produced subtropical vegetation (☞ pp. 12–13). The present sparse vegetation dates from the last ice age about 18 000 years ago.

Many ancient species have become extinct, and two distinct floras now exist. On the inland mountains, some earlier species have survived and later spread to ice-free oases. The Antarctic Peninsula and adjacent islands have been colonised by species from South America.

## Plants

The extreme conditions make Antarctica a habitat in which only the hardiest plants can survive. Very few species have been recorded on the 2% of the continent that is ice-free. They include about 150 lichens, a dozen mosses, some fungi and a liverwort.

*Antarctic plants vary from single-celled algae which stain the snowfields red in summer (left); to lichens which live on and inside rocks (centre); to only two flowering plants (right).*

There are only two flowering plants, which grow only on the Antarctic Peninsula and adjacent islands, at low levels and on warm north-facing sites. Here, there are also many more lichens, often on rocks in the coastal salt spray zone or near bird colonies, where there are more nutrients.

The ice sheet itself is virtually sterile, though algae can grow in coastal snowfields which melt during the summer. Inland, where the high mountains poke through, lichens and occasional mosses are found. In 1978, scientists made the amazing discovery of lichens, fungi and algae actually growing inside rocks in the Dry Valleys of Victoria Land. The rock is transparent enough to allow sufficient light to filter through and it is a far warmer, less windy environment than the surface. As a result, some of these communities have survived for thousands of years.

## Animals

Animals find it even harder than plants to survive in Antarctica. The only permanent residents are invertebrates, mostly microscopic. The largest is a wingless midge only 12 mm long. There are many species of single-celled animals called protozoans, and tiny nematode worms are some of the most successful inhabitants. Even more common are tardigrades, minute caterpillar-like animals less than 0.25 mm long.

 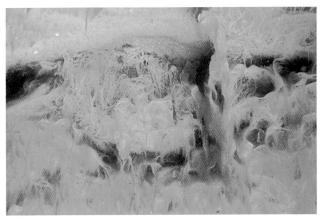

*Deep Lake (left) in the Vestfold Hills is a freshwater lake. Its bed is covered with a thick mat of algae (above).*

Compared to other regions, insects are scarce and small in Antarctica. Only 67 species have been recorded, and most are less than 2 mm long. Most of them are parasites, like lice which live in the feathers and fur of birds and seals, where they are protected from the harsh climate for much of the time. Collembola (springtails) are the only free-living insects. They feed on algae and fungi, and remain dormant in winter.

Mites, which belong to the spider family, are the commonest land animals. One of them, which is only 0.3 mm long, is the world's most southerly indigenous animal. It has been found as far south as 85°.

## Life in lakes

Not all Antarctic animals are as tough as that, however, and the many lakes in the ice-free oases offer a less demanding habitat. Even so, most freshwater lakes have a very simple ecosystem. For example, Deep Lake in the Vestfold Hills supports only a few single celled plants and animals, which in turn feed a tiny crustacean about 2 mm long.

## Visitors

While Antarctica is tough for residents, it is popular with visitors. Eleven species of seabirds and three of penguins nest on the ice-free land, most returning to the same rookery site each year. About 5 million Adélie penguins, the most abundant, build their nests of small stones on the bare rock close to the shore. Other birds, like snow petrels, nest in rock crevices and on ledges in mountains as far as 300 km from the coast.

But by March or April each year the visitors are gone, leaving only the hosts of minute battlers to endure the frigid darkness of winter.

*Snow petrel's nest in a rocky crevice.*

*Adélie penguins build their nests out of small stones on the bare rock.*

# Habitats 2: Ocean circulation and biological zones

I N THE Southern Ocean there is a complicated pattern of surface currents, vertical circulation and seasonal ice cover which influences what lives where in its vast expanse.

## Surface currents

Close to the Antarctic continent the winds are mainly from the east, while further north in the furious fifties and roaring forties the winds are mainly from the west. The surface currents of the ocean are driven by these winds.

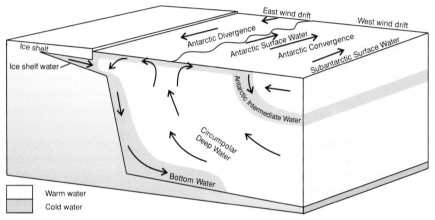

Warm water
Cold water

*There are complex vertical and horizontal currents in the Southern Ocean.*

The Antarctic Divergence separates these zones of the east and west wind drift (☞ diagram).

## Vertical circulation

As the pack ice freezes in autumn and winter, a layer of very saline water is formed underneath it (☞ p. 26). This water is heavy and cold, so it sinks. It then moves north along the continental shelf and into the depths of the ocean as Antarctic Bottom Water.

The Antarctic Surface Water is also cold and moves north. At the Antarctic Convergence it meets warmer Subantarctic Surface Water flowing south, and sinks below it. This produces a sharp temperature gradient of up to 2°C across the Convergence. Between these two cold north-moving masses a warmer, nutrient rich mass of Circumpolar Deep Water moves south, and wells up towards the surface around the Antarctic Divergence.

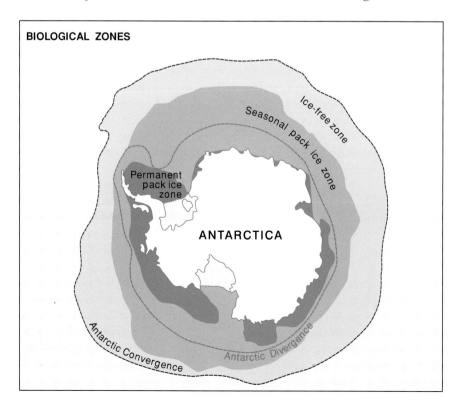

BIOLOGICAL ZONES

*The Antarctic Convergence is a natural barrier that contains within it three major biological zones, related to these currents and to the seasonal formation of pack ice.*

## Ice cover

The seasonal advance and retreat of the pack ice also interacts with these horizontal and vertical currents in the ocean. In winter it extends beyond the Antarctic Divergence, and reduces the upwelling of the Circumpolar Deep Water in that region while increasing the flow of Antarctic Bottom Water. In summer it retreats, leaving a layer of cold less salty water which reinforces the northward flow of the Antarctic Surface Water.

There are three main biological zones in the Southern Ocean, related to these three factors.

## Ice-free zone

The ice-free zone covers most of the west wind drift south from the Antarctic Convergence to the northern limit of the seasonal pack ice. This zone is rich in nutrients but low in productivity. It is like a marine desert, with only a few species of fish and squid in its deep blue waters, and virtually no krill.

## Seasonal pack ice zone

In contrast, the seasonal pack ice zone is a zone of abundance. In spring and summer the ice edge retreats quickly southwards, releasing algae trapped within it and triggering phytoplankton 'blooms' (☛ p. 50). This primary productivity is enriched by the nutrients upwelling in the warmer Circumpolar Deep Water. Its abundance supports most of the diversity and productivity of the Antarctic marine ecosystem (☛ p. 47).

*The advance and retreat of the pack ice reinforces the ocean circulation, and creates a seasonal zone of great abundance.*

*Amphipods (above) are small crustaceans which live in the rich and colourful sea floor environment (left) below the pack ice.*

## Permanent pack ice zone

The permanent pack ice zone, including the ice shelves, is close to the coast of the continent. Here, in contrast to the other two zones, most life is on the ocean floor, where it is as rich and colourful as any tropical reef. Under the ice there are few surface feeders, and so most of the phytoplankton falls to the bottom. There it slowly decomposes and provides a continuous supply of food for seaweeds, crustaceans, corals, sea spiders, sponges and anemones.

# Habitats 3: Ocean, the most hospitable and abundant

O F ALL the habitats of the Antarctic ecosystem, the seasonal ice zone is the most abundant. It supports the greatest diversity of species, with the largest numbers of each species.

## Phytoplankton

This great diversity and productivity is based on phytoplankton, a varied group of tiny free floating plants. In spring and early summer their numbers increase rapidly, producing 'blooms' like a thick pea soup which can cover thousands of square kilometres of the ocean. These blooms provide a food source which is 300–400 times more concentrated than normal for a variety of zooplankton (tiny animals), especially copepods and krill, which in turn provide food for fish, seals, whales and penguins. Not surprisingly, zooplankton grow rapidly, increasing their body weight by around 5% a day over the short summer.

## Krill

Although not the most abundant species of zooplankton, krill is the most commercially important (☛ p. 90) and so its biology is the best known. Surprisingly, it is poorly adapted to its environment. It is heavier than water and has to work hard just to keep afloat. For this, it has five pairs of legs for swimming, and also several more that form a net to filter its food.

Krill spawn in summer, and mature females can do so twice a season. They lay 2000–3000 eggs each time and the eggs sink into deep water where they are carried southwards on the currents to the edge of the continent. There they hatch into larvae, which go through several stages as they gradually rise, emerging on the surface as adults in two or three years.

Krill live a long time for plankton, up to seven years in the laboratory and probably four or five in the sea. In winter, they feed on algae on the underside of the pack ice (☛ p. 50).

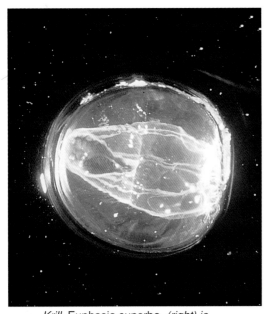

*Krill*, Euphasia superba, *(right) is a large member of the Antarctic zooplankton. It feeds on many different kinds of phytoplankton like the diatom (above).*

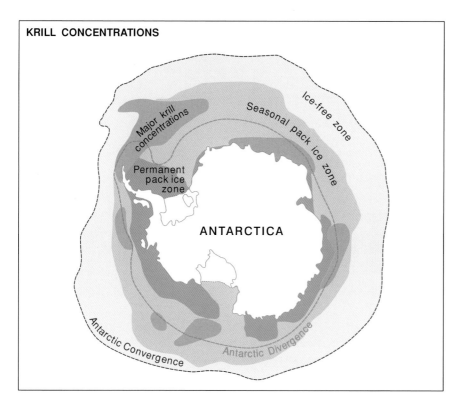

**KRILL CONCENTRATIONS**

Ice-free zone

Seasonal pack ice zone

Major krill concentrations

Permanent pack ice zone

ANTARCTICA

Antarctic Convergence

Antarctic Divergence

*Major concentrations of krill around the Antarctic continent occur mostly within the seasonal ice zone. Krill prefer colder water and are not found beyond the Convergence.*

They shrink on this sparse diet, but make up for it the following summer when the phytoplankton blooms once more.

## Krill eaters

It is estimated that the Southern Ocean contains around 400 to 650 million tonnes of krill, the staple diet of fish, seals, birds and whales. The biggest eaters are seals, consuming 130 million tonnes a year. About 100 million tonnes a year is taken by birds, 90% of it by penguins. Baleen whales consume about 60 million tonnes and fish a much smaller amount.

## Crabeater seals

Crabeater seals are now the single biggest consumers of krill, accounting for 63 million tonnes a year. This is more than all the remaining baleen whales put together. Their numbers have increased enormously in the last 50 years as whales were hunted almost to extinction, and there are now about 12–15 million. For the whales to make a comeback the crabeater population may have to fall, but it is not clear how this could happen.

*Crabeater seals have displaced baleen whales as the biggest consumers of krill.*

## Whales

The most numerous whale is now the minke, smallest of the baleen whales, with a population of about 750 000. It is estimated that there are only 1000 of the giant blue whales left, out of a pre-hunting population of 200 000. All Antarctic whales breed in tropical or subtropical waters, and migrate south to feed for the summer. Only minke, killer and blue whales inhabit the seasonal ice zone where the most abundant food supplies are found.

# Habitats 4: Ice, the half year, halfway house

T HE area of pack ice varies enormously during the year and at its greatest extent covers nearly 20 million km² (☛ p. 26). Although it forms a barrier to shipping and a dangerous environment for humans, it is home to millions of seals and penguins.

## Winter pack ice

During spring and summer the seasonal pack ice zone is the most abundant habitat of the Antarctic ecosystem (☛ p. 55). During winter, the pack ice is almost as inhospitable as the continent itself (☛ p. 52), but some species of large animals can survive in it.

## Emperor penguins

The most remarkable is the emperor penguin, which actually breeds on the pack ice in winter. It is the only species of bird which never sets foot on land. About 195 000 pairs form 40 colonies in the same 'place' each year

Though clumsy on land, penguins are in their element underwater, and can dive to 500 metres.

around the Antarctic coast. About 12 000 of these come to Auster rookery amongst some spectacular grounded icebergs near Mawson station.

Breeding begins in March, when the new ice is barely thick enough to support their weight. Elaborate courtship rituals take about six weeks and the female lays a single egg in mid-May. She then departs to spend the winter at sea.

Chicks lose their fluffy down to become fully fledged in five months.

Left behind, the male scoops the egg onto his feet and under a thick fold of skin, and settles down to wait. For 65 days, in temperatures down to −45°C and blizzards up to 200 km/h, he incubates the egg. He keeps as still as possible and huddles close to his fellows to conserve body heat (☛ p. 49). During this time he eats nothing, and only has snow to drink. As a result, male penguins lose 40% of their body weight. Some cannot endure the fast and abandon their eggs and head for the sea to feed.

For those that stick it out, relief comes with the return of the females in mid-July, just as the chick is hatching. With amazing accuracy, partners

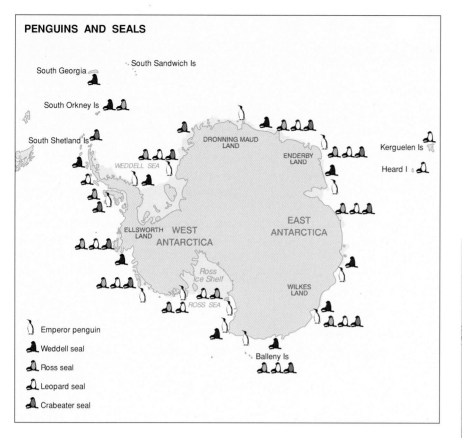

**PENGUINS AND SEALS**

South Georgia
South Sandwich Is
South Orkney Is
South Shetland Is
DRONNING MAUD LAND
ENDERBY LAND
Kerguelen Is
Heard I
WEDDELL SEA
ELLSWORTH LAND
WEST ANTARCTICA
EAST ANTARCTICA
Ross Ice Shelf
WILKES LAND
ROSS SEA
Balleny Is

Emperor penguin
Weddell seal
Ross seal
Leopard seal
Crabeater seal

*There are about 40 emperor penguin colonies around the continent, and the four species of seals occur at varying densities in the pack ice.*

*Weddell seals pup on the pack ice in spring.*

recognise each other's calls amongst the thousands of others, and the chick is transferred to the mother's feet and pouch. While she feeds it regurgitated fish on demand, the male is free to find his first meal in four months. But this is still a two-day journey across 80 km of pack ice to the open sea. When he gets there, he may have to dive to over 300 metres to find food.

## Chicks' rapid growth

After three weeks the males return to relieve the females. By the next changeover the chicks are big enough to be left in creches so that both parents can bring food to them. By mid-December, they have reached 60% of their adult body weight, shed their fluffy down for a smart dinner suit and are ready to try their luck in a new environment, the sea. Although 30% or more don't make it to this stage, those that do have a good chance of living at least 20–30 years.

Emperors are so big they need nine months to complete their breeding cycle. They can just fit this into the period of the annual freezing and break-up of the pack ice. But to do so, the males must endure a harsh winter fast, and the chicks have to risk hatching very early in spring.

## Seals in the pack ice

Crabeater seals also spend the winter on the pack ice, and breed on it in spring. Weddell seals live underneath the ice during winter and chew holes in it so they can breathe. In spring the females haul out to give birth to their pups, which they suckle for only six weeks before weaning. The other Antarctic seals — the Ross and leopard seals — spend winter at the edge of the pack ice, but they too breed on it in spring. These seals eat krill, squid and fish. Leopard seals are predators as well, the terror of penguins, especially Adélies, and young crabeater seals.

*Leopard seals are predatory on other seals and penguins.*

# Subantarctic islands 1: Plants and mammals

**SUBANTARCTIC ISLANDS**

Bouvet I

Prince Edward I

Marion I

South Georgia    South Sandwich Islands

Crozet Islands

South Orkney Islands

Kerguelen Islands

South Shetland Islands

McDonald I

WEDDELL SEA

Heard I

WEST ANTARCTICA    South Pole    EAST ANTARCTICA

ROSS SEA

SOUTHERN OCEAN

Macquarie I

**E**IGHT islands or groups of islands in the Southern Ocean lying close to the Antarctic Convergence are classed as subantarctic. Even within this group there are marked differences in climate and landscape.

The most southerly islands, Bouvet Island and the South Sandwich group, are almost entirely ice covered. South Georgia and Heard Island, both just south of the Antarctic Convergence, are mountainous, with permanent ice caps and snow fields. Kerguelen and Marion are lower, with only small glaciers. Macquarie and the Crozet islands are north of the Convergence and are completely ice-free.

All lie within the zone of the west wind drift (☞ p. 54) and are windy, wet and cold all year round. All are 1000 km or more from the nearest continent.

## Plants and animals

There are more native plants than on the Antarctic continent, but the number of species is still limited by climate and isolation. Overall there are 72 flowering plants, plus several hundred mosses, liverworts, lichens and fungi. There are no trees or shrubs, and the tallest plants are tussock grasses about 1–2 metres high. But there is much more variety, from big moss

*Sheltered valleys on Macquarie Island support quite luxurious vegetation.*

*Harems of female elephant seals are dominated by the much larger males.*

and peat beds on South Georgia to occasional gullies of ferns and broad-leaved 'cabbage' plants on Macquarie Island.

There are also more animals including 210 species of insects and 144 of spiders, as well as nematodes, earthworms, collembola, mites and other microscopic species. However, there are still only a few vertebrate residents although there are millions of visitors.

## Elephant seals

The largest are the southern elephant seals which breed on all the subantarctic islands. Adult males are 6–7 metres long and weigh up to four tonnes. The males fight for control of harems of up to 50 females when they haul out on the beaches in September to give birth to their pups.

The females fast for 30 days while suckling their pups. By then the pup is big enough to fend for itself at sea but its mother will normally have lost about 200 kg in weight. The dominant 'beachmaster' males may spend 90 days ashore without food, defending their territories sometimes to the death and breeding with as many females as possible. After a few months at sea to regain condition, both males and females return to their beaches in March to moult, There are about 750 000 elephant seals in the three main breeding groups on South Georgia, Kerguelen and Macquarie Islands.

## Fur seals

Antarctic fur seals which breed on islands south of the Antarctic Convergence, are smaller but twice as numerous. Like the elephant seals, they breed in huge harems. Unlike them, fur seals do not have sufficient blubber for the females to be able to fast while suckling their pups. So throughout the summer they go to sea for several days to feed on krill and squid to replenish their milk supply. As a result the pups take much longer to wean — about 115 days. Combined with the value of their fur, this long breeding season ashore made them especially vulnerable to sealers, but now their numbers are increasing rapidly.

*Male elephant seals fighting for dominance of a harem of females.*

## Subantarctic islands 2: Birds

*There are about 10 million crested penguins like macaronis and royals on subantarctic islands.*

B Y FAR the most numerous vistors to subantarctic islands are the millions of penguins and sea birds which breed on them each year.

Six species of penguins nest in varying numbers on the various island groups, though Adelies are found only on the coldest islands, Bouvet and the South Sandwich group. Chinstraps are found mainly on the southern and rockhoppers on the northern islands. King, macaroni and gentoo penguins are the most widely distributed.

### King penguins

King penguins are especially abundant on Crozet, Macquarie and Marion Islands, with a total population of about 2 million. Like the emperors, king penguins are too big to fit their breeding cycle into one short summer. But instead of incubating the egg over winter and so being able to rear a chick each year (☛ p. 58), king penguins raise two chicks in three years.

### Breeding cycle

In the first year of this cycle, breeding starts in October. The eggs are laid on the island beaches in November and hatch from mid-January. Both parents share incubation and chick care in shifts and can easily bring food from the sea. By mid-April the chicks have reached 90% of adult body weight but are not yet fledged. They huddle together through the winter with only infrequent feeds from their parents.

*This king penguin rookery at Lusitania Bay on Macquarie Island has about half a million birds.*

Next spring, with plenty of food available again, they grow quickly, moult and leave the colony. Their parents spend this second summer at sea then return to breed, laying eggs which hatch in March. These new chicks are also abandoned in winter, with much less chance of survival than their larger siblings. But if they succeed, their parents spend the whole of the following (third) summer feeding them so they are ready to leave the colony by autumn. Then for the parents the cycle begins again the following October.

## Smaller penguins

King penguins share the beaches with several species of smaller penguins which can manage to fit their whole breeding cycle into a single summer. Macaronis, one of the crested penguins, nest in their millions on South Georgia, Heard, Marion and Crozet Islands. Rockhoppers, the smallest southern penguin, are often found with macaronis, especially on Heard Island. Gentoos, the fastest swimmers of all, breed mainly on South Georgia.

## Seabirds

While penguins crowd the beaches and nearby slopes, seabirds nest on the cliffs and higher ground each spring. Around 35 species visit the subantarctic islands. They range from the magnificent wandering albatross, which flies thousands of kilometres to feed, to gulls, cormorants and terns, which hunt closer inshore. Most return to the same sites each year. Some, like the albatross, mate for life. In addition five species of land birds live all year round on South Georgia, Kerguelen and Marion Islands.

*Light-mantled sooty albatross and chick on Macquarie Island.*

## Introduced animals

As well as these residents and visitors, there are also animals introduced by humans. Cats, rats, mice and rabbits compete with native birds on many islands. There are reindeer on South Georgia and sheep on Kerguelen Island, brought by settlers. Only Heard Island is free of such intruders.

*Feral cats on Macquarie Island prey on young birds.*

# It's a dog's life

*Belgrave Ninnis and his team on Mawson's 1911 expedition. They later disappeared down a crevasse.*

F OR nearly a century, sledge dogs have been used in Antarctica. They served expeditions of many nations, but in recent years they have been replaced by motor vehicles for most purposes. For this reason, and because they can damage the environment, the member nations of the Antarctic Treaty (☞ p. 87) agreed to remove them by April 1994.

Sledge dogs were first used in Antarctica by Carsten Borchgrevink in 1898–1900. Roald Amundsen reached the South Pole in 1911 with their help (☞ p. 35) and Sir Douglas Mawson began the Australian tradition of dog sledging the same year (☞ p. 39). This was revived when ANARE (the Australian National Antarctic Research Expeditions) was established after World War II (☞ p. 84). It was maintained until 1993 when the last dogs were removed from Mawson station, after almost 43 years of service.

## Huskies

Huskies — as sledge dogs are often called — come from the Arctic, where there are four distinct types, from Labrador, Greenland, Alaska and Siberia. They are well adapted to the cold and windy conditions, with thick woolly coats. In blizzards they curl up nose to tail with their backs to the wind. They sometimes get covered in snow, but providing they have a hole to breathe through, it keeps them warm.

*Oscar Wisting's team was the first to reach the South Pole with Amundsen in 1911.*

Huskies are strong, energetic dogs and a team of ten or twelve can pull a loaded sledge and two people 50 km or more in a day. One person usually rides on the back of the sledge to use the brake if needed. The other calls directions to the lead dog — 'Le-e-e-e-eft' or 'Rt, Rt, Rt, Rt' — or sometimes runs ahead to lead them in the right direction. Though they are very friendly to humans, huskies sometimes fight amongst themselves, and there is always a pecking order in a team. Family groups often make up the best teams and bitches, who are more obedient, make excellent lead dogs.

*The first ANARE dog team on Heard Island.*

## Australia's huskies

The first ANARE dogs were 31 mixed Labrador–Greenland huskies. They were part of a pack brought out in 1948 by a French expedition, which failed to reach the continent due to exceptionally heavy pack ice that year. So the expedition leader asked Sir Douglas Mawson to help arrange board for the dogs in Australia, instead of taking them back to France. They spent the winter at Melbourne Zoo and by next summer the pack had doubled, so the French gave half to Australia.

Most were sent to the first ANARE station on Heard Island over the next two years. By 1954 there were 85 dogs, and 30 were taken to the continent when Mawson station was established.

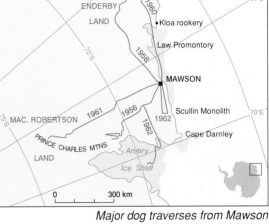

*Major dog traverses from Mawson in the 1950s and 1960s.*

## Exploring by dog sledge

In the next three summers, dog teams helped map the Prince Charles Mountains and explore its geology. Husky Massif in the Aramis Range, over 400 km south of Mawson, was named in their honour. In 1958, 13 dogs were flown to Enderby Land, over 600 km west of Mawson. They returned overland pulling sledges for a party of surveyors and geologists. In the early 1960s, dog teams combined with vehicles surveyed the Amery Ice Shelf to the east, and explored the southern Prince Charles Mountains.

From the 1970s onwards, the Mawson huskies were mainly used for recreation and for survey work of emperor penguin colonies on the sea ice. The winter trip to Kloa rookery, 350 km west of Mawson, was an annual event until the dogs' final departure.

## From South Pole to North Pole

In 1957, 26 Mawson huskies were given to Sir Vivian Fuchs for his Transantarctic expedition during the International Geophysical Year (☞ p. 95). They were the first dog teams to reach the South Pole since Amundsen's.

When the last huskies left Mawson in 1993 they went to an Outward Bound school in Minnesota, USA. Later a team reached the North Pole, proving once again their strength and endurance.

*'Blizzard' was born at Commonwealth Bay on Mawson's expedition. He soon had to endure the harsh conditions he was named after.*

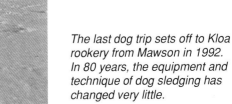

*The last dog trip sets off to Kloa rookery from Mawson in 1992. In 80 years, the equipment and technique of dog sledging has changed very little.*

# Creating a comfort zone 1: Clothing and food

A NTARCTICA is the only continent with no native human inhabitants. So all the essential life support systems people need to
survive have to be imported from outside. These include clothing,
food, shelter and energy.

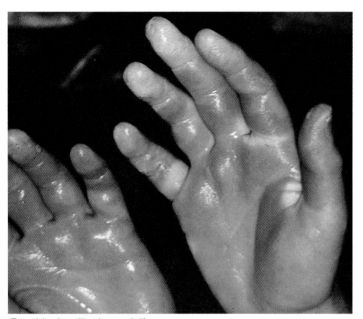

*Frostbite is still a hazard, if proper clothing is not worn.*

## Clothing

Clothing is the first line of defence against the hostile environment. If a person is active, or in shelter, the body's natural heat is sufficient to keep warm providing it can be retained by well insulated clothing. The best way is to wear many layers of clothing that trap the air between them.

Today's well dressed Antarctic expeditioner might wear acrylic thermal underwear, then a woollen shirt and trousers. A fibre-pile or wool-len sweater would come next, then close-woven cotton 'ventile' trousers and jacket, or a one-piece down-filled 'freezer suit' with an outer windproof fabric. Several pairs of woollen socks with felt bootliners and thick-soled leather or canvas boots are needed for the feet; woollen gloves topped by fleece-lined canvas or fur mit-tens for the hands; a fur hat or balaclava and hood for the head; plus a face mask and goggles.

Earlier explorers used the same multi-layer principle, but materials were heavier and not so well designed. British expeditions used a special very finely woven cotton 'Burberry' cloth for their outer windproof anoraks and trousers. Fur suits were popular with Scandinavian expeditions like Amundsen's, and some even used fur underwear.

*Captain Scott in 'Burberry' clothing (above). Modern expeditioners wear down-filled 'freezer' suits (left), windproof 'ventiles' (centre right) and fleece-lined jackets (right) to protect them from wind and cold.*

## Hypothermia and frostbite

In Antarctica cold temperatures are almost always combined with strong winds. The windchill factor (☞ p. 21) can lower the effective temperature so much that no amount of clothing can eliminate the risk of hypothermia. This happens when a person loses heat more quickly than their body can generate it from food or physical activity. Gradually their internal, core temperature drops, which causes unconsciouness and eventually death as the heart stops. Frostbite is a more local effect of cold, usually striking fingers and toes, noses and ears which are most exposed. This causes the blood vessels to contract so that the tissues slowly die and turn white.

## Food

In such a hostile and isolated environment, food is important for morale as well as for health. In earlier years, scurvy due to lack of vitamin C from fresh food was a real danger. Meals were a monotonous sequence of canned or salt meat, dried vegetables, biscuit, porridge, bread and cakes. Occasionally there was seal or penguin meat, and rarer still, penguin eggs. Now, with freezers, refrigerators and warm stores, chefs can create varied and nutritious menus all year round from the food brought in on the annual resupply ship.

*Sledging rations (left) on Mawson's 1911–14 expedition were very spartan, compared with the mouth-watering food (above) chefs can now prepare for special occasions.*

In the field the diet was even more restricted. It was based on pemmican, a mixture of dried meat, fat and cereal in a compressed block. It was boiled with water and plain biscuit for the evening meal of 'hoosh'. Although it was easily prepared and a good source of energy, it was very monotonous. Now, a whole range of freeze dried foods takes its place.

## Creating a comfort zone 2: Shelter and energy

SHELTER of any kind, even an igloo or ice cave, can make the difference between life and death when the windchill factor rises. Energy for heat and light in winter, for telecommunications and entertainment, provides comfort and civilisation.

Most early buildings in Antarctica were wooden huts like Borchgrevink's at Cape Adare (☛ p. 30) with little insulation. They provided shelter from the wind but the inside temperature was still mostly below freezing, even if they were heated.

Scott's second expedition hut at Cape Evans was primitive and cramped. An occasional bath in a tin tub took care of personal hygiene. Clothes were worn out rather than washed. Acetylene gave poor light and there was almost no privacy. A gramophone and books provided recreation, with parties on special occasions like birthdays or Midwinter. There was no link with the outside world at all, until the relief ship arrived to take the expedition home.

### Permanent bases

After World War II, bases became more permanent and special building techniques were developed. The AANBUS (Australian Antarctic Building System) used for Australia's stations is typical. Prefabricated panels with a polystyrene core, inner reflective surfaces and tough enamelled outer walls are bolted onto strong steel frames. Buildings can be erected quickly in the short summer, and partitions, services and furniture fitted in the winter.

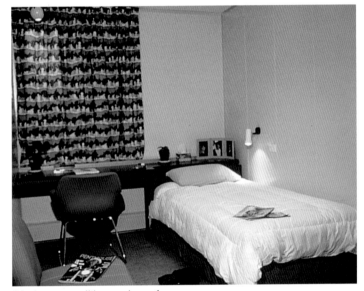

*Modern expeditioners have far greater comfort and privacy (above) compared to the cramped sleeping quarters of Scott's Cape Evans hut in 1911 (right).*

The 'Red Shed' at Mawson is built on the AANBUS system.

The 'Red Sheds' or living quarters at Australia's stations provide individual bed-sitting rooms for each person. There are hot showers and a laundromat, a modern kitchen and communal dining and lounge rooms, video and games rooms, a library and a photographic dark room. A satellite link provides telephone, facsimile and data services to Australia and the rest of the world.

## Energy

Power comes from electricity generated by diesel engines that use up to 600 000 litres of fuel each year. Exhaust heat is used to warm water for central heating, while the water itself is made in electric powered snow or ice melters. All these services are carried round the station in insulated, heated pipes.

## In the field

But some things have not changed. The polar pyramid tent is still the best shelter for field expeditions. In Scott's day it was very cramped for the usual three occupants, who also shared a communal reindeer skin sleeping bag. It often froze so solidly they had to chip their way in with an ice axe every night! Now, larger double skinned tents and down sleeping bags are much more comfortable.

Primus stoves are still the simplest and most reliable source of heat for cooking and for melting snow and ice for water.

For more permanent field accommodation, demountable huts like the fibreglass 'Apple' — which can be extended to a 'Melon', a 'Zucchini' or even a 'Cucumber' by adding sections in the middle — have been developed. They provide more space, shelter and comfort than a tent, but can easily be moved around by helicopters or vehicles.

Pyramid tents are still best suited to the windy conditions of Antarctica. Modern design makes them less cramped than Edward Wilson's drawing from Scott's 1910–12 expedition.

Fibreglass 'Apple' huts now used for field camps are much more comfortable and spacious.

# Getting there

All ships sailing to Antarctica run the risk of violent storms (above) in the Southern Ocean, which can cause enormous damage to cargo, like these helicopters (below), reduced to scrap metal when a lashing broke.

A NTARCTICA, the world's most remote continent, can only be reached by crossing the world's stormiest ocean.

Even the shortest route, from South America to the Antarctic Peninsula, crosses Drake Passage where the winds and waves of the Southern Ocean surge with terrifying force round Cape Horn. And then for most of the year ships face an almost impenetrable barrier of pack ice before they can reach the continent itself.

## Early ships

The first ships to brave these seas were Captain Cook's *Resolution* and *Adventure* in 1772 (☞ p. 29). *Resolution* was only 34 metres long and *Adventure* even smaller. Their wooden hulls were vulnerable to ice and they had only limited power and manoeuvrability under sail. It was nearly another century before stronger steel hulls replaced wooden ones in most Antarctic ships.

Shape is as important as strength if a ship is caught in the pack ice. Amundsen's ship *Fram* was originally designed to be carried close to the North Pole locked in the ice. So she had a saucer-shaped hull which would be squeezed upwards onto the ice as the pressure grew. But Shackleton's *Endurance*, with a deeper, narrower hull, was crushed and sunk (☞ p. 36).

## Distances by air

| | |
|---|---|
| Christchurch–McMurdo | 3920 km |
| Johannesburg–Molodezhnaya | 4500 km |
| Punta Arenas–Antarctic Peninsula | 1500 km |
| Davis–Casey | 1400 km |
| Davis–Mawson | 630 km |

## Distances by sea

| | |
|---|---|
| Hobart–Casey | 3400 km |
| Hobart–Mawson | 5500 km |
| Hobart–Davis | 4800 km |
| Perth–Davis | 4700 km |

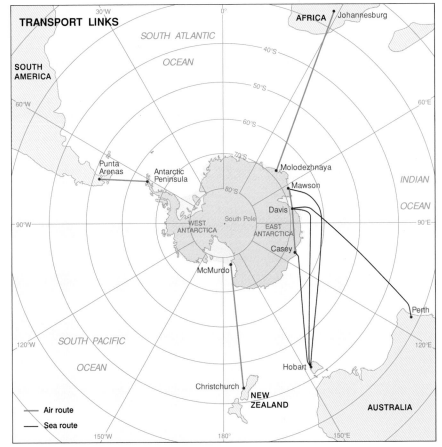

TRANSPORT LINKS

— Air route
— Sea route

## Icebreakers

Operation Highjump in 1946 (☞ p. 40) was the first expedition to use modern icebreakers. Their specially strengthened hulls and powerful engines enabled them to cut a path through pack ice up to several metres thick. The United States and Russia now use nuclear powered icebreakers.

*Breaking through the pack ice.*

Australia has a specially designed icebreaker and research ship, *Aurora Australis*, which was launched in 1989. It is used to resupply the stations each summer, and to carry out marine science in the Southern Ocean and pack ice en route. Modern stations need thousands of tonnes of fuel, food and equipment brought in each year for their life support systems, and rubbish and empty fuel drums taken away. If something is forgotten, there's no corner store to get it from!

Sometimes even a powerful icebreaker cannot get as far as the shore. Then the pack ice makes a natural wharf for unloading cargo onto sleds and over-snow vehicles (☞ p. 74) which ferry it ashore, while passengers go by helicopter. In January and February the pack ice usually melts enough to allow ships to reach the stations to unload directly.

## Air travel

Aircraft obviously provide much quicker and more comfortable access to the continent than ships. A voyage lasting 20 days can take only half as many hours by air. The first intercontinental flights were made by the United States in 1955–56 from Christchurch in New Zealand to McMurdo Sound in the Ross Sea. An ice runway was built to take heavy wheeled aircraft, and it is now used by huge Hercules to supply the US, New Zealand and Italian bases in this area.

*Hercules aircraft at McMurdo.*

Russian aircraft fly to Molodezhnaya from South Africa, and the British, Chileans and Argentinians access their bases on the peninsula by air also. Aircraft now make Antarctica accessible for much more of the year. The first winter fly-in to McMurdo starts in August, when the sun is barely over the horizon.

# Getting around 1: Early expeditions

I N THE early days of Antarctic exploration man, dog and horse power were the main ways of getting around. Horses were the least successful, and were only used by British explorers who at first did not understand how to manage dogs.

*Scott relied on manhauling.*

Amundsen proved that dogs were the best and most adaptable form of transport in the early years, and they were used by several nations until 1993 (☞ p. 64). Manhauling, though in Scott's opinion the noblest way to go, is so slow and exhausting in Antarctic conditions that it is really only a last resort.

## The first motor vehicles

Early expeditions also experimented with cars and tractors. These were unreliable enough in temperate climates and on good surfaces, let alone in the extreme conditions o f Antarctica. In 1907 Shackleton took the first car to the continent, but its narrow wheels bogged in soft snow. Scott tried tracked vehicles with more success, until they broke down mechanically.

Mawson had the most original idea on his Australasian Antarctic Expedition of 1911–14 (☞ p. 38). He had planned to take an aeroplane to Antarctica but it was damaged during a demonstration in Australia. So he left the wings behind and used it as an 'air tractor' to tow sledges until the engine seized.

*Shackleton relied on horses.*

*The first aircraft — without its wings — never got off the ground, but was used to pull sledges.*

## Overcoming engineering problems

It took many years of engineering development to design motor vehicles that could stand the stresses of Antarctic travel. There are three main problems.  First, in very cold temperatures metals become brittle and so chassis and suspensions crack easily travelling over rough ice and snow. Second, lubricating oil freezes and fuel gets waxy and hard to pump and vaporise, so engines will not start. Third, vehicles have to be able to handle soft snow and hard ice, as well as *sastrugi*, wind-whipped snow waves like frozen surf up to 3 metres high.

The first vehicles to overcome these problems were three half-track Citroen trucks used by an American expedition in 1933. On the Transantarctic Expedition of 1957–59 Edmund Hillary succesfully used Ferguson farm tractors. Vivian Fuchs drove Sno-cats, the first purpose built, independently tracked over-snow vehicles used in Antarctica (☛ p. 94). From the 1960s onwards, motor vehicles provided greater speed and comfort than dogs — though they are often harder to start in the mornings!

*The first car had narrow wheels and got bogged in soft snow.*

# Getting around 2: Modern transport

THERE is now a variety of specially designed vehicles that make Antarctic travel faster and safer on the ground. Ski-equipped aircraft can carry cargo long distances, and helicopters make even mountain tops accessible.

*Skidoos*

## Skidoos

For personal transport with light loads, skidoos or motor toboggans are ideal. They carry one or two people and, with driving tracks at the back and a steering ski at the front, they can handle soft snow easily. On hard ice, whether on land or sea, four-wheeled agricultural motor bikes or 'quikes' go better. They are also more economical and easier to maintain.

## Hägglunds

For longer trips in harsher conditions, 'Hägglunds' vehicles are very versatile. These are specially built in Sweden for military patrol work in the

Arctic. They have two fibreglass cabs linked together and run on rubber tracks. They can carry four or five people and all their equipment and supplies for a week or more. They have a top speed of about 50 km/h on smooth ice and snow, and have excellent traction in difficult conditions. They even float, if they go through a crack on the sea ice! Their main limitation is fuel capacity for long journeys. Even when towing fuel sleds their maximum range is about 1000 km.

## Tractors

Dog teams have been replaced for long inland traverses by huge bulldozer/tractors, like Caterpillars or the Russian Kharkovchankas which weigh over 30 tonnes. They are modified with wider tracks for lower ground pressure, and also need special fuel systems to cope with the thin cold air of the inland ice sheet up to 4000 metres high.

Each tractor can tow a train of six or eight sleds weighing up to 80 tonnes. One carries a living caravan, usually a converted cargo container. Another has a generator van with a diesel engine running 24 hours a day to pro-

*Caterpillar tractor*

vide heating and power for instruments. The others carry fuel, food and equipment for the journey. This may take four to six months and cover many thousand kilometres. Most expeditions have two or three such tractor trains, which can travel at 6–8 km/h. But in deep snow, two or three tractors may have to be hitched to each train, so sometimes it can take a day to cover only a few kilometres.

## Navigation

Navigating in Antarctica is rather like being in a ship at sea. This impression is reinforced by the way the vehicles roll over the *sastrugi*. Expeditions use the same techniques of astro-navigation, using the sun or stars to fix position. Now this is being replaced by navigation with GPS (Global Positioning System) using satellites (☛ p. 41).

Because the south magnetic pole is so close, compasses have to be specially adjusted to give reliable directions. Empty fuel drums and beer cans on bamboo poles are used to mark known routes. These can be 'seen' by radar carried on vehicles and show a safe way home, even in blizzards.

## Hazards

The main hazards of ground travel in Antarctica are crevasses, which can be up to 20 metres wide and hundreds deep (☛ p. 25). They are often covered with snow bridges which conceal their dangers. Like reefs in the ocean, they are ready to trap the unwary.

Powerful tractors can usually pull each other out, but dog teams can be swallowed whole, as Mawson found to his cost (☛ p. 39). Modern echo-location instruments can sometimes detect crevasses. But in unexplored territory great caution is needed even today.

*The hazards are still the same.*

## Helicopters

Now, helicopters provide a much safer and quicker form of transport for field expeditions, especially for scientists who need to sample a wide range of ice, rock or biological sites in a short time. But even helicopters are limited by the weather. Whiteout (☛ p. 21) is especially dangerous because it is impossible to judge the height above the snow when landing.

*Quikes and helicopters give scientific expeditions much greater range and mobility.*

# Working in Antarctica 1: Laboratory science

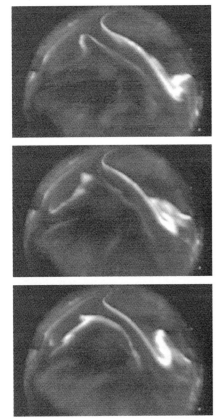

**A**NTARCTICA is a unique scientific laboratory. Some research is also done inside laboratories at stations, mainly on problems in physics and medicine.

## Auroras

One area of special interest is the study of auroras, the winter light shows that have fascinated visitors to the continent for over a century. Auroras are caused by interactions between the sun and the earth's atmosphere hundreds of kilometres out in space. As well as radiating heat and light energy, the sun also emits a continuous stream of electrically charged sub-atomic particles known as the solar wind.

The earth's magnetic field creates a 'magnetosphere' which surrounds it in space. The magnetosphere is distorted by the force of the solar wind, because the charged particles cannot cross the magnetic field. Instead, they are channelled towards the magnetic poles. There they enter into the upper atmosphere and interact with its gases. This interaction produces different wavelengths of light, which we see as auroras. Blue light is produced by nitrogen and red and green by oxygen.

*A sequence of images (above) at four second intervals taken by the auroral video camera (right) shows how quickly auroras change.*

*The earth's magnetic field is flattened by the force of the solar wind and directs charged particles to the poles, where auroral activity is concentrated.*

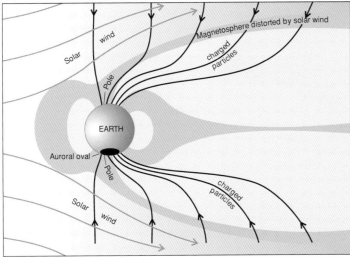

Because solar wind particles can only penetrate the earth's magnetic field at the poles, auroras are concentrated around these areas, which are known as the auroral ovals. For a variety of reasons the southern auroral oval is more accessible than the northern. This means that many Antarctic and subantarctic stations are in an ideal position to study auroras.

Special laboratories have been set up, with automatic video cameras that can photograph the whole sky at night to record auroral activity. In addition, scientists are investigating the different factors that cause auroras. They measure variations in the earth's magnetic field; they monitor the dynamics of charged particles making up the solar wind; and they measure changes in the ionosphere — the level of the atmosphere where interaction with the solar wind takes place.

## Cosmic rays from outer space

As well as the charged particles of the solar wind, space is full of other particles of cosmic radiation from more distant sources. These spiral through the magnetic fields of the galaxy as well as the earth, and can be detected with special instruments. This gives physicists information about our galaxy that no other optical, x-ray or radio astronomy techniques can provide. Antarctica is an ideal place to study these cosmic rays. At the Mawson laboratory, some of the detectors are in a cellar dug 11 metres into solid rock, which only the most energetic radiation can reach.

Outside the protective layers of the earth's atmosphere, cosmic radiation can be very damaging to satellites, space ships and to possible future space colonies. Cosmic radiation is the 'weather' of outer space. Scientists need to understand its behaviour to be able to give accurate 'forecasts' for space travel in future.

*Cosmic rays penetrate deep underground to instruments at the Mawson observatory.*

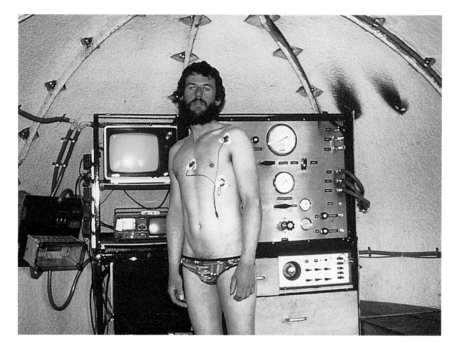

*Expeditioners help doctors study the effects of isolated living in Antarctica — or possibly space.*

## Medical research

Antarctica has other links to space too. Expeditioners are one of the most isolated groups on earth, with no physical contact with the outside world for up to ten months. They have to contend with bitter cold and long periods of darkness. They live and work in a restricted environment and are forced into close contact with only a few companions (☛ p. 82).

These are almost the same conditions in which people would live in space colonies. So Antarctica provides a laboratory where doctors can study the physical and psychological stresses of such a lifestyle. In particular, they are investigating the capacity of expeditioners to resist infection. This seems to be reduced by factors like low levels of light and vitamin D intake during winter. This lowered resistance means many expeditioners catch colds or flu when newcomers arrive on the first ship or aircraft in spring.

# Working in Antarctica 2: Field science

LABORATORY research can be done all year round but most field research takes place in summer. The population of Antarctica quadruples between October and March as scientists fan out to glaciers, mountains, islands and ice shelves to gather as much data as they can in the short time available.

## Adélie penguins and krill consumption

Adélie penguins are huge krill consumers and they nest in their millions on the coast and offshore islands each year (☞ p. 53). Scientists study their breeding and feeding habits as part a program coordinated by the Commission for the Conservation of Antarctic Marine Living Resources (☞ p. 90) to assess the effect of harvesting krill on krill predators.

The main technique used is to weigh the adults before and after they feed their chicks. Australian scientists have set up an ingenious automated weighing system at an Adélie colony near Mawson station. A fence guides incoming adults over a weighbridge that electronically records the number of their implanted identity tag, their weight, and the date and time. When the same bird leaves it is weighed again and the difference automatically recorded. Breeding pairs are identified, so scientists can calculate the food input for each chick over the season. At this colony, adults deliver about 20 tonnes of food to rear 400 chicks each season. From this data, the krill consumption of all the Adélie colonies around the continent can be estimated.

## Underwater research

Both Adélie and emperor penguins swim long distances and dive deep to find food for themselves and their chicks. Scientists attach radio locaters and dive depth recorders to selected birds, to get a better idea of where they go and what they do between visits to the colony. As well, divers equipped with thick wet or dry suits can join them under water to study how they behave in their natural element, and also the amazing diversity of life on the sea floor (☞ p. 57).

*Being weighed by hand can be a rather uncomfortable experience for a penguin.*

*Much easier for both scientists and subjects is an automatic weighbridge across the only easy access to the penguin colony.*

*Divers studying the behaviour of seals and penguins underwater enter a magical environment under the ice.*

Collecting fish or other sea creatures for examination is difficult. Out of the water, their tissues freeze in the much colder air. So warm, insulated storage is needed to get them to the laboratory for study.

## Studying the ice sheet

Glaciologists have the opposite problem. The cores they drill from several thousand metres deep in the ice sheet need constant refrigeration on the surface and in the laboratory. They use these cores to analyse the gases and other materials trapped in the ice at different depths. This gives information about climate and other environmental conditions in earlier centuries (☞ pp. 104–105).

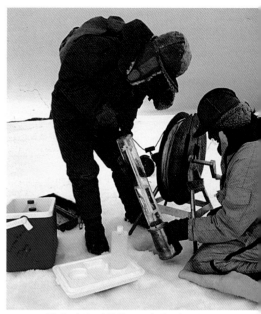

*Biologists drill through the ice to sample water and organisms in the lake below.*

*Glaciologists have to pinpoint ice stakes on remote glaciers, and then take care not to fall into a crevasse when remeasuring their position.*

Glaciologists also study the behaviour of glaciers and the inland ice sheet. To study how fast a glacier moves, they put stakes at different points across its direction of flow, and measure their position accurately using satellite fixes. In later years, finding the same stakes and remeasuring their position enables the rate of ice flow to be calculated. Coupled with radar measurements of ice thickness (☞ p. 23) the total outflow of ice towards the sea can be estimated. Automatic weather stations set up by inland traverses record temperatures and snowfall accumulation. Over many years the rates of ice accumulation and outflow can be compared to determine whether the ice sheet is growing or shrinking.

## Understanding Antarctica's geology

Although there is little rock above the surface of the ice in Antarctica, it provides evidence of the evolution of Gondwana and the more recent geological history of the continent (☞ pp. 10–11, 14–15). Geologists collect rocks and fossils from remote mountains, and make maps and aerial surveys to trace the location of similar kinds of rocks. Because rock outcrops are so scattered in Antarctica, helicopters help geologists make the most of their time in the field.

But like all Antarctic scientists, their work has barely begun at the end of the short summer season. The examination of samples and analysis of results takes many more months before a paper can be published to share new discoveries with other scientists.

*For a geologist, even the 2% of the continent not covered by ice can reveal fascinating discoveries.*

# Working in Antarctica 3: Support and logistics

*The power house is the heart of a station's life support systems.*

ALTHOUGH the main reason expeditions go to Antarctica today is to do scientific research (☛ p. 76–79), the scientists make up less than 25% of the staff of any expedition. This is because life support systems on Antarctic stations are now just as complex as anywhere else, and there is also a variety of special needs for transport, communication and maintenance.

## Maintaining electricity supply

It takes a lot of people just to keep the station running. The most essential job is to maintain the electricity supply for heating, lighting, communications and workshops, as well as for scientists' instruments. Most stations have a bank of diesel engines to generate electricity and transmission lines to supply all buildings. Although many automatic control systems are fitted, the diesel mechanics and electricians need to be skilled trouble shooters to keep failures to a minimum. Other expeditioners help by taking turns to check the power house at night, and report any unusual instrument readings.

## Water supply

Water is the next most important requirement, and so the station plumber is also a key figure. Water is made by melting snow or ice and is pumped around the station in heated, insulated pipes. If this system fails, usually in the harshest winter weather, a frozen pipe can take days to repair.

*Water for cooking, washing and heating buildings, and electrical and other services, are carried round the station in raised trays to keep them above the snow drifts in winter.*

The water supply is also crucial for guarding against the greatest hazard on an Antarctic station — fire. In the very dry and windy environment fires spread rapidly, so expeditioners are trained in fire fighting. The fire chief is usually the head electrician, who is responsible for maintaining all the alarm systems — and who gets the blame if one goes off accidentally in the middle of the night!

## Vehicle maintenance

As well as keeping the power house running, the mechanics are also responsible for maintaining all the vehicles at the station and in the field. They have plenty of tools and spares in a heated workshop at the station. But if a vehicle breaks down in the field it can be a different story. Then the

*Mechanics have to cope with difficult conditions maintaining vehicles in the field.*

safety of the party may depend on a mechanic's ability to find the problem and carry out repairs in conditions where bare hands stiffen to wooden claws in a few minutes and thawing them out in time to prevent frostbite is pure agony. Sometimes the breakdown cannot be fixed without extra equipment or spares, so a radio call back to the station has to be made.

## Radio communications

Radio is the lifeline of field parties, and until recently of communications with the outside world as well. So radio operators and technicians also play key support roles. Operators set up 'skeds' at pre-arranged times to keep contact with field parties as well as listening round the clock for emergency calls. Technicians maintain the equipment they need to do this, especially the arrays of radio aerials that festoon most Antarctic stations. These are needed to transmit and receive signals over the long distances between Antarctica and the rest of the world.

Nowadays satellite systems are replacing radio for this purpose. They can provide telephone, fax and data links that are faster, more reliable and more private than telex or voice transmissions by radio.

*Radio technicians (above) need a good head for heights to maintain the aerials; but satellite dishes, protected by geodesic domes (left) can now provide more reliable long-distance communications.*

## Buildings, stores and logistics

Building maintenance, like all outside work, can be cold, painful and awkward because of the need for heavy protective clothing. Construction workers also have special problems like getting concrete to set, not freeze, in sub-zero temperatures and handling equipment safely in high winds.

As well as all the people who work at keeping a station running, there are many others who work at keeping *them* running. Some of the most important are of course the chefs, who keep everyone fed. But they also rely on the supply and logistics staff to make sure they have food in the larder to cook. Hundreds of people back home order, pack and dispatch all the stores needed by the stations each year. Equally important are the ships' crews and aircraft pilots who make sure they get there.

Many different tasks have to be coordinated in a very tight time frame to keep the stations supplied. Ingenuity, versatility and stamina are essential qualifications for the people who keep *them* running. Everyone has to be an expert at their own job, and willing to lend a hand with all the unexpected tasks that crop up when living in an isolated, harsh environment.

*Construction workers pouring concrete for building foundations.*

# Community life

**W**HY do people go to Antarctica, and how do they get on together when they are there? The early explorers went to make new discoveries, for national glory, for personal fame and commercial fortune. None of these reasons is valid now.

*Expeditioners often have to work together on physically tiring jobs in uncomfortable conditions.*

But the lure of the world's last great wilderness with its awe inspiring beauty is still strong. Scientists still find many fascinating problems to research (☛ pp. 76–79). All expeditioners are experts at their jobs and many welcome the chance to work in a challenging environment. For many it is an avenue for promotion, for a few it becomes a major part of their career. For some it is an escape from difficult work or family situations, for others a chance to save money. For almost all, it is an adventure.

## Coping with stress

For anyone who goes to Antarctica for more than a few months there are costs as well as rewards. First there is the separation from friends and family. Although some stations have satellite telephone services, this does not wholly make up for the lack of physical contact for long periods. Second, there are physical hardships like the cold and the lack of light in winter, and the endless buffeting of strong winds. Third, there is the stress of living in confined quarters with a small unchanging group of companions, 24 hours a day and seven days a week. Fourth there is the lack of recreation opportunities, both indoor and outdoor. No cricket, tennis or swimming and at most only one TV channel!

So how do people cope and stay sane? Some don't, and if they are lucky they can leave before winter. On some early expeditions people went mad. Now expeditioners are selected not only for their professional skills but also for their psychological stability and their social adaptability. The kind of person best able to cope with the stresses of Antarctic life seems to be tolerant, self-sufficient, cooperative and fairly conformist.

*Recreational excursions or 'jollies' to explore the environment help to build morale.*

## Morale and management

Even well adjusted expeditioners experience changes of mood during the year. In summer, everyone is very busy, and ships and aircraft bring letters from home so the isolation is not too intense. After the last ship leaves at the end of summer, people enjoy the sense of a smaller more intimate community with more freedom of movement. This usually maintains morale until Midwinter, which is a major community celebration. It is in the dark days of July and August that depression can set in. People withdraw into their own private worlds, tempers get frayed and work performance suffers. With the arrival of spring people look forward to the ship or plane home. Then, as that date approaches, they often try to cram into the last weeks all the things they had meant to do in the past year.

*Midwinter is the most important festival of the Antarctic calendar, and brings the community together with a magnificent banquet followed by plays and songs.*

Managing a community with these stresses can be a real challenge for the station leader. As well as handling the administration, station leaders must resolve conflicts, encourage social activities, maintain their own energy and enthusiasm, and support others with their personal problems. Above all, station leaders need to keep the respect and loyalty of expeditioners.

## Women in Antarctica

Early expeditions were exclusively male and often based on military-style discipline. Women were excluded because of the harsh physical conditions and lack of privacy. Since the 1970s, women have gained more access to this as to many other male-dominated work areas, but the competition for jobs is strong. All expeditioners must be expert and versatile and in some technical areas, few women have the broad experience needed. When they do make it, they often face social and sexual pressures in such a confined and traditionally male culture. This is slowly changing as women's abilities become more accepted, but they are still in a very small minority.

*Diana Paterson was the first woman station leader in Antarctica.*

A survey of 19 nations with winter expeditions in Antarctica in 1992 showed that only seven of them employed women, and they made up less than 10% of over-winterers. Many more stay for the summer only, especially scientists, who make up over 50% of the women who go to Antarctica each year. They also work as radio operators, doctors and chefs, though there are few mechanics or tradespeople, and even fewer station leaders. Only Germany and Australia have employed women in this role. The first was at Australia's Mawson station in 1989.

## 50 years of ANARE

I N 1947, the Australian National Antarctic Research Expeditions (ANARE) was established. Sir Douglas Mawson played a major part in persuading the government to set up this organisation for ongoing science and exploration.

HMAS Labuan, *a naval landing craft, putting the first ANARE team ashore at Heard Island in 1947.*

Australia claimed over 42% of the continent as a result of Mawson's own expeditions in 1929–31. It was important to reinforce this claim by establishing bases. In addition, as a geologist Mawson believed that the continent could hold valuable mineral resources.

### ANARE program

The initial program of ANARE was to re-open Mawson's old station on Macquarie Island, establish a new one on Heard Island, and find a site for a station on the continent in George V Land, the part closest to Australia (☛ map on p. 6). By 1948 the first two goals were achieved but not the third. Expeditions to the islands concentrated on scientific work, especially meteorology, sending observations back to Australia by radio to help weather forecasters. In addition surveying, biology, auroral and cosmic ray physics, and glaciology (on Heard Island) programs were developed (☛ pp. 76–79).

*Mawson station was proclaimed on 13 February 1954. Philip Law, first Director of ANARE, is beside the flag.*

*Macquarie Island is Australia's only permanent subantarctic station.*

### Dr Philip Law

In 1949 Dr Philip Law became Director of ANARE. He was determined to establish a station on the continent, but he needed an ice-strengthened ship. Eventually he found a suitable Danish ship, *Kista Dan*, for charter and in 1954 set up Mawson station. It was not in George V Land close to Australia, but thousands of kilometres further west in Mac. Robertson Land. This was partly because it was closer to the existing station at Heard Island. The main reason was that aerial photographs from Operation Highjump showed an ideal site there — a natural harbour surrounded by ice-free land.

## Mawson station

The ten men led by Bob Dovers who spent 1954 at Mawson were the first Australians to winter in Antarctica since 1913. Mawson is now the longest continually operating station on the continent. The first buildings were wooden and aluminium huts or 'dongas', but gradually laboratories, stores, a power house and workshops were built. Private sleeping quarters and a mess with a library and recreation area came next. Beer and wine was provided for special occasions like Midwinter (☛ p. 83). Expeditioners also brewed their own beer or 'homers', a tradition which continues today.

## Casey and Davis Stations

In 1957, as part of its contribution to the International Geophysical Year (IGY) (☛ p. 94), ANARE established another station in the Vestfold Hills. It was named Davis after the captain of *Aurora* on Mawson's 1911–14 expedition (☛ p. 39). While scientists at Mawson explored the inland ice sheet and mountains, those at Davis concentrated on the ice-free oasis and its many lakes at their back doorstep.

*One of the first buildings erected at Mawson was a wooden hut recycled from a Norwegian expedition.*

In 1959 the United States handed over its Wilkes station, established for the IGY, in the Australian Antarctic Territory. It was gradually buried by ice and snow, and so a new station, Casey, was built on a better site nearby. To keep it above the drifts, it was built in sections on stilts linked by a covered corridor. This unique 'caterpillar' design was very successful until the stilts began to rust, so a third station was built and opened in 1988.

*Casey station was built above ground on stilts to prevent it being buried in drift, but has since been replaced.*

## ANARE today

In 1966 Philip Law retired after 18 years as Director of ANARE. In this period ANARE became established as a leader in Antarctic science. It has maintained this position since then with better equipment and more scientists. The number of expeditioners has grown from the first ten men in 1954 to about 100 men — and women — in winter and up to 400 in summer.

In addition, Australia has become a leading player in the Antarctic Treaty and other international forums concerned with the management and protection of the continent (☛ pp. 86–93). As a result, the work of ANARE has changed its focus from exploration in the early days to science and conservation as the main priorities of the future.

*Brewing 'homers' is a long standing ANARE tradition.*

# The Antarctic Treaty

## The Antarctic Treaty — a summary

**ARTICLE I**: Antarctica shall be used for peaceful purposes only. All military activities, including weapons testing, are prohibited. However military personnel and equipment may be used for scientific purposes.

**ARTICLE II:** Freedom of scientific research and cooperation shall continue.

**ARTICLE III**: Scientific information, personnel, results and research plans shall be freely exchanged and international cooperation encouraged.

**ARTICLE IV:** The Treaty and any activities carried out under it do not endorse, support or deny any territorial claim. No new claims shall be made while the Treaty is in force. No member state is required to recognise any other's territorial claim.

**ARTICLE V:** Nuclear explosions and the disposal of radioactive waste are prohibited.

**ARTICLE VI**: The Treaty applies to all land and ice shelves below 60°S, but not the high seas, which are subject to international law.

**ARTICLE VII**: Any member state may send observers, with due notice, to inspect any station, installation or equipment. All members shall give notice of expeditions, stations and military personnel and equipment active in Antarctica.

**ARTICLE VIII:** Observers and scientists shall be under the jurisdiction of their own states.

**ARTICLE IX**: Member states shall meet periodically to exchange information and take measures to further Treaty objectives, including the conservation of living resources. Meetings shall be open to member states that conduct substantial scientific research in Antarctica.

**ARTICLE X**: Member states will discourage any activity by any nation which is contrary to the Treaty.

**ARTICLE XI**: Disputes are to be settled by negotiation, or ultimately by the International Court of Justice.

**ARTICLE XII**: After 30 years, any member state may request a review of the operation of the Treaty.

**ARTICLE XIII**: The Treaty is open to any member of the United Nations, or by invitation of all the member states.

**ARTICLE XIV**: The United States is the repository of the Treaty and is responsible for providing copies to all member states.

BEFORE World War II over 20 nations had been involved in research and exploration in Antarctica. In some cases this was due to individual initiative and curiosity. Other nations had claimed parts of the last continent for military or strategic reasons or in the hope of exploiting its natural resources.

These nations were Argentina, Australia, Chile, France, New Zealand, Norway and the United Kingdom. Their claims are unequal. The largest is Australia's claim to over 42% of the continent. Three claims, those of Argentina, the United Kingdom and Chile, overlap, while a sixth of the continent is unclaimed.

After the war this situation was complicated further when both the USA and the USSR increased their interest in Antarctica. Although neither was a claimant nation, this threatened to bring all the tensions of the Cold War to the only continent which had so far escaped armed conflict. In 1948 the USA proposed to the claimant nations that some sort of international trusteeship should be set up to govern Antarctica. But only New Zealand was prepared to give up its claim in order to make this possible.

## Science leads the way

Fortunately, scientists are often better at international cooperation than politicians. In 1957–8 the International Geophysical Year created a worldwide research program with special emphasis on the polar regions. Twelve nations, including the USA and the USSR, set up cooperative science programs in Antarctica. This led to another conference on the future of Antarctica in 1958. All the twelve nations involved in the IGY realised that science could be the key to defusing the political tensions and reaching a workable agreement.

It took 60 meetings to agree on a treaty which was signed by the twelve nations in 1959. The treaty then had to be ratified by the parliaments of these nations, and finally came into force in June 1961.

## The Antarctic Treaty

The Antarctic Treaty is a surprisingly short and simple document, but it is one of the most successful international agreements ever made. It recognises that 'it is in the interest of all mankind that Antarctica shall continue to be used for ever for peaceful purposes and shall not become the scene or object of international discord'. The key to achieving this aim is Article IV, dealing with territorial claims. It makes this a non-issue by freezing existing claims, without making judgement on their validity, and by prohibiting new claims. No nation has to recognise anothers claim.

Any member of the United Nations can accede to the Treaty. Provided they carry out 'substantial research activity' in Antarctica, they can become Consultative Parties with the same status as the original twelve nations. Forty-two nations have now signed the Antarctic Treaty of which 26 are Consultative Parties (☛ right).

## Consensus decisions required

The Consultative Parties meet every two years to make new decisions on how best to manage the continent. A number of Conventions regulating particular activities have been agreed to over the past 30 years (☛ pp. 88–93). All decisions must be by consensus, which means they can take a long time to reach. But overall, members have been prepared to put their concern for Antarctica to remain 'a land devoted to peace and science' above their own national interests.

The Antarctic Treaty has been criticised as a 'rich man's club' by some third world nations. However, since 1991 it has provided a unique agreement for the peaceful use of the continent. The Antarctic Treaty system was further strengthened in 1991 by the adoption of the Protocol on Environmental Protection (Madrid Protocol) (☛ p. 93).

## Antarctic Treaty Parties — 1994

| Party | signed | |
|---|---|---|
| Argentina* | 1961 | CP |
| Australia* | 1961 | CP |
| Belgium* | 1960 | CP |
| Chile* | 1961 | CP |
| France* | 1960 | CP |
| Japan* | 1960 | CP |
| New Zealand* | 1960 | CP |
| Norway* | 1960 | CP |
| Russia* | 1960 | CP |
| South Africa* | 1960 | CP |
| United Kingdom* | 1960 | CP |
| United States* | 1960 | CP |
| Poland | 1961 | CP |
| Denmark | 1965 | |
| Netherlands | 1967 | CP |
| Romania | 1971 | |
| Brazil | 1975 | CP |
| Bulgaria | 1978 | |
| Germany | 1979 | CP |
| Uruguay | 1980 | CP |
| Colombia | 1981 | |
| Italy | 1981 | CP |
| Papua New Guinea | 1981 | |
| Peru | 1981 | CP |
| China | 1983 | CP |
| India | 1983 | CP |
| Cuba | 1984 | |
| Finland | 1984 | CP |
| Hungary | 1984 | |
| Spain | 1984 | CP |
| Sweden | 1984 | CP |
| Republic of Korea | 1986 | CP |
| Austria | 1987 | |
| DPR of Korea | 1987 | |
| Ecuador | 1987 | CP |
| Greece | 1987 | |
| Canada | 1988 | |
| Switzerland | 1990 | |
| Guatemala | 1991 | |
| Ukraine | 1992 | |
| Czech Republic | 1993 | |
| Slovak Republic | 1993 | |

\*    Original signatory
CP   Consultative party

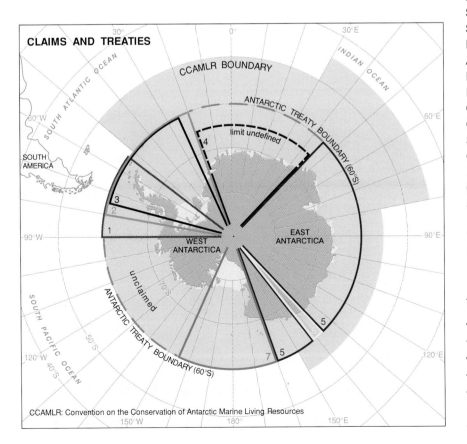

CLAIMS AND TREATIES

CCAMLR BOUNDARY

ANTARCTIC TREATY BOUNDARY (60°S)

limit undefined

SOUTH AMERICA

WEST ANTARCTICA

EAST ANTARCTICA

unclaimed

ANTARCTIC TREATY BOUNDARY (60°S)

CCAMLR: Convention on the Conservation of Antarctic Marine Living Resources

Territorial Claims

| | |
|---|---|
| 1 | Chilean Antarctica |
| 2 | British Antarctic Territory |
| 3 | Argentine Antarctica |
| 4 | Dronning Maud Land (Norway) |
| 5 | Australian Antarctic Territory |
| | Adélie Land (France) |
| 7 | Ross Dependency (New Zealand) |

# Conservation of living resources 1: Seals and whales

O VER the past 30 years the Antarctic Treaty System has provided an effective tool for managing the continent and surrounding oceans. A number of conventions have been added to the Treaty in this time. Most are concerned with conservation of living resources, under Article IX (☛ p. 86).

In 1964, the Agreed Measures for the Conservation of Antarctic Fauna and Flora set out basic rules for running stations. It was realised that humans compete with animals and plants for the few ice-free areas in Antarctica, and so it is important they damage the environment as little as possible.

## Protection for seals

In the 1960s there was some concern that commercial sealing might revive and again threaten several species of Antarctic seals that were slowly recovering from the wholesale exploitation of the 19th century.

Fur seals had been virtually wiped out since the industry started in 1800–01 when 112 000 skins were taken. By 1822 James Weddell (☛ p. 29), estimated that 1.2 million seals had been slaughtered. From 1870 the industry was uneconomic because so few seals were left, and when commercial sealing finally ended in 1912, around 3 million fur seals had been killed. Elephant seals were the next target. They were harvested for their oil rather than their skins. By the 1950s when that industry also failed, over 1 million seals had died.

To protect the remaining seals, a Convention for the Conservation of Antarctic Seals was negotiated and signed in 1972. It sets very low limits on catches of some seals, and entirely prohibits others. Commercial sealing has never resumed, but this convention began what has become a very successful strategy of the Antarctic Treaty; to establish rules to manage a resource when there is no immediate pressure to exploit it. This makes it far easier to reach agreement.

### 1964 Agreed Measures for the Conservation of Antarctic Fauna and Flora

- killing, wounding, or capturing any native mammal or bird is prohibited except with a permit
- permits will only be given for
  - scientific collections
  - essential food for men or dogs
  - living specimens for zoos
- dogs shall not be allowed to run free
- helicopters, vehicles, explosives or firearms must not be used within 200 metres of any colony
- areas of outstanding scientific interest shall be designated as Specially Protected Areas where all activities are prohibited without a permit
- no non-indigenous species shall be imported without a permit

### 1972 Convention on the Conservation of Antarctic Seals

- applies to all species of seals in all seas south of 60°S latitude
- yearly catch limits are set of
  - Crabeater 175 000
  - Leopard 12 000
  - Weddell 5 000
  subject to periodic review
- killing of Ross and fur seals is prohibited
- killing of any seals between 1 March and 31 August, and of any seals in special reserves, is prohibited

*Several conventions have increased the protection of seals and other animals.*

## Whaling

Antarctic whaling is not regulated by the Antarctic Treaty, but by the International Whaling Commission (IWC) which covers all the world's oceans.

Like sealing, whaling also followed a pattern of 'boom and bust' exploitation. First humpback, then blue, fin, sei and minke whales were hunted almost to extinction. Only 1% of the original stocks of blue whales, 3% of humpbacks and 30% of fin whales remain. Since Antarctic whaling began in 1904, 1.3 million whales weighing 70 million tonnes have been killed.

Whaling has been far harder to control than sealing because a few nations have a continuing commercial interest in it. When the IWC was set up in 1946, it tried to enforce limited seasons, minimum sizes and other controls to halt the decline in whale stocks. But little was known about whale ecology so there were no clear scientific limits to exploitation.

In 1972 the United Nations Conference on the Environment called for a ten-year moratorium on commercial whaling. Due to opposition by Russia and Japan, the two main whaling nations, it was not adopted by the IWC until 1982. In 1992 Norway and Iceland tried without success to have the moratorium lifted.

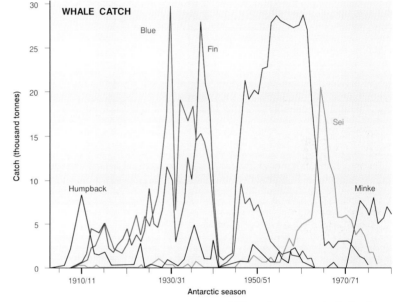

*Different species of whales have been exploited in succession as each stock is exhausted.*

In Antarctica, the Japanese continue to kill about 300 minke whales a year for scientific purposes. In 1994, on the initiative of France and Australia, the IWC declared an Antarctic whale sanctuary.

*Japanese ships still kill whales for scientific purposes. This ship was hunting off Davis station in February 1992.*

## Conservation of living resources 2: Fish and krill

THE next Antarctic resources to be threatened by commercial exploitation were fish and krill. In the 1960s many countries extended their territorial waters to the 200 mile limit. This drove the world's ocean fishing fleets to more remote fishing grounds, including Antarctic waters.

### Antarctic fisheries

Russian trawlers began commercial fishing in the south Atlantic in the late 1960s, concentrating on 'Antarctic cod'. By 1970 they were taking over 400 000 tonnes of fish a year, mainly from around South Georgia. When catches dropped to a few thousand tonnes a year, other species of icefish and toothfish were targeted, with the same result.

This follows the same pattern of 'boom and bust' exploitation as sealing and whaling. Fish catches (☛ graph) have fluctuated widely as each species was exploited. The main reason for this is that Antarctic fish are long-lived, grow slowly and take a long time to reach maturity and breed. This means they cannot be as heavily harvested as quicker growing and breeding species.

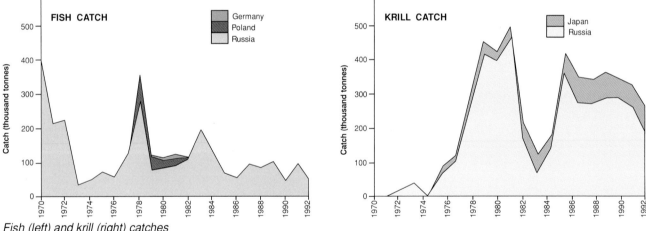

*Fish (left) and krill (right) catches have fluctuated as different stocks were exploited. They have now stabilised at sustainable levels. Russia takes by far the biggest share.*

### Krill harvesting

Krill, for example, have a shorter life span and a twice yearly breeding cycle (☛ p. 56). So they are much more productive and can sustain a higher yielding fishery. This was begun in the 1970s, mainly by Russian and Japanese trawlers. By 1982 the annual catch was over 500 000 tonnes. While this is only a small fraction of the estimated 500 million tonnes of krill in Antarctic waters, there are many other species which depend on it (☛ p. 57). It is calculated that 50 million seals, 850 000 whales and 400 million seabirds eat 17 million tonnes of fish, 20 million tonnes of squid and 250 million tonnes of krill a year.

### Ecosystem management

In the 1970s the Antarctic Treaty nations became concerned about the increasing exploitation of marine resources. Also, they realised that any convention to manage these resources, especially krill, would have to take into account the impact of harvesting on other species.

The Convention on the Conservation of Antarctic Marine Living Resources (CCAMLR), which came into force in 1982, broke new ground by creating an ecosystem approach to resource management. That is, it not only aims to conserve the 'target' species of any fishery, it also takes into account the impact of fishing on the other animals that feed on and compete with the target species.

To do this, CCAMLR had to be applied not just within the 'political' boundary of the Treaty area at 60°S, but within the 'natural' boundary of the Antarctic Convergence (☞ map on p. 87). So it also broke new ground in being a convention of a Treaty which applies outside the Treaty area.

*Krill is at the centre of the Antarctic marine ecosystem. Harvesting it will affect many other species.*

## Quotas

CCAMLR has tried to set catch limits that will ensure a sustainable fishery. For fish, the catch is now about 100 000 tonnes a year, only 25% of the harvest 20 years ago. CCAMLR also imposes quotas and bans on particular species and fishing zones. For krill, there is a limit of 1.5 million tonnes a year, divided between several regions. In this way, harvesting can be controlled and the ruthless, and commercially disastrous, over-exploitation of the sealing and whaling industries can be prevented.

## Research for the future

But to make the ecosystem management concept work, much more information is needed about the interactions of the various species. An ecosystem monitoring program has been set up to detect changes in the populations of animals that are not commercially harvested. This program has identified a number of species that are particularly sensitive to the supply of krill for their food.

Adélie penguins are one of the species being studied (☞ p. 78). The results of this research will be very important in setting realistic quotas in future. It will also help to convince the main fishing nations like Russia, Japan and Poland that these quotas are legitimate, if they try in the future to increase their harvest, especially of krill.

### 1982 Convention on the Conservation of Antarctic Marine Living Resources

- applies to all populations of fin fish, molluscs, crustaceans, and all other species including birds found south of the Antarctic Convergence, which form part of the Antarctic marine ecosystem

- any harvesting of resources shall be conducted in accordance with the following principles of conservation
  - prevention of reduction of any population below a sustainable level
  - maintenance of ecological relationships between harvested, dependent and related populations of living marine resources
  - prevention of changes to elements of the marine ecosystem that cannot be reversed over two or three decades

- conservation measures will be determined by the Commission and will be binding on all members 180 days after notification

- a scientific committee will advise the Commission on criteria for conservation measures, and carry out research on the status and population trends of marine living resources, and assess the direct and indirect impact of harvesting on them

## Conservation vs exploitation of mineral resources

I T WAS hard enough for Antarctic Treaty nations to reach agreement on the conservation of living resources. The really tough problem was how to regulate the exploitation of mineral resources if it ever occurred.

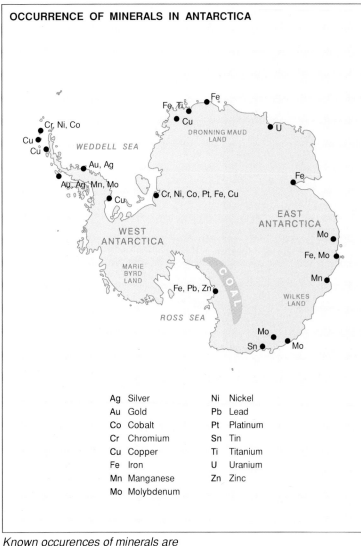

### OCCURRENCE OF MINERALS IN ANTARCTICA

| | |
|---|---|
| Ag | Silver |
| Au | Gold |
| Co | Cobalt |
| Cr | Chromium |
| Cu | Copper |
| Fe | Iron |
| Mn | Manganese |
| Mo | Molybdenum |

| | |
|---|---|
| Ni | Nickel |
| Pb | Lead |
| Pt | Platinum |
| Sn | Tin |
| Ti | Titanium |
| U | Uranium |
| Zn | Zinc |

*Known occurences of minerals are widely scattered and inaccessible.*

In fact, very little is known about the mineral resources of Antarctica because most of them are buried deep in the ice. Only 10% of the ice-free areas have been accurately mapped, and only 1% surveyed for minerals. There are deposits of low grade iron and coal in the Prince Charles Mountains (☛ p. 14) and higher grade coal in the Transantarctic Mountains. Some indications of oil have been found by research drilling in the Ross Sea. However, the possible existence of mineral deposits in Antarctica is mainly based on comparisons with similar geological formations in Africa, Australia and other continents which were once part of Gondwana.

### Control over mining needed

Nevertheless, there was a concern that uncontrolled exploration and mining could cause political and environmental problems. So in 1982 Antarctic Treaty nations began negotiations on a Convention on the Regulation of Antarctic Mineral Resource Activities (CRAMRA). It took until 1988 to reach a consensus. The two major problems were how to prevent environmental damage, and how to resolve territorial issues. Conservation groups like Greenpeace were totally opposed to any mining activity in Antarctica. They fought long and hard to persuade member nations to ban it entirely, and declare Antarctica a World Park. They were not successful in this, but did manage to ensure that CRAMRA included strict environmental controls.

### Ownership of mineral resources

The territorial issues related mainly to payment for ownership of mineral resources. Normally a 'royalty' payment is made by a mining company to the owners of the ground from which minerals are extracted. Seven nations claim pieces of Antarctic 'ground', but other nations do not recognise those claims. In the negotiations on CRAMRA, Australia as the largest claimant nation had a special interest in how royalties would be paid and distributed.

The final agreement was that all royalties would be paid to the CRAMRA administration, not to the nation claiming the ground from which the

minerals were taken. However this would not in any way affect the validity of the claim, under Article IV of the Treaty. Royalties would be distributed to fund research, but claimant nations would not get any special advantages from the exploitation of minerals in their claims.

## Mining convention abandoned

Although CRAMRA was signed at the Treaty meeting in 1988, to come into force it had to be confirmed by all the claimant nations. In May 1989 both Australia and France decided not to do this. CRAMRA was very much a compromise agreement between the strongly pro-mining nations like America, Britain and Germany, and those most influenced by the conservation movement, including Australia and France. In the end, Australia decided that neither the system of royalty payments nor the environmental controls were adequate.

This meant that CRAMRA could not be enforced and six years of work over eleven lengthy meetings was wasted.

## Replaced by Madrid Protocol

Instead, Australia and France proposed a comprehensive conservation convention. In two years of intense lobbying, first Belgium and Italy, then gradually other member nations, gave their support. Finally, the Protocol to the Antarctic Treaty on Environmental Protection was signed at the Treaty meeting in Madrid in 1991. This marked a major change in the attitudes of Treaty nations to the value of conserving Antarctica, but it could only have been reached through the conflict over CRAMRA.

The Madrid Protocol defines Antarctica as a natural reserve devoted to peace and science and prohibits any mineral activity except research. As well, it sets out detailed requirements for environmental impact assessments of all human activities. It strengthens the existing measures for the conservation of flora and fauna. It sets up new standards for waste disposal and management, and for prevention of marine pollution. It also outlaws non-indigenous animals from the continent, and as a result all sledge dogs had to be removed by 1 April 1994 (☞ p. 64).

### 1991  Madrid Protocol on Environmental Protection

- designates Antarctica as a natural reserve devoted to peace and science
- establishes environmental principles for the conduct of all activities
- gives priority to scientific research, especially research which contributes to understanding the global environment, and requires tourism and private expeditions to follow this principle
- prohibits activity relating to mineral resources, other than research
- subjects all activities to prior assessment of their environmental impact
- establishes procedures for
  - environmental impact assessment
  - conservation of fauna and flora
  - waste disposal and waste management
  - prevention of marine pollution
  - special area protection and management
- prohibits the introduction of non-indigenous animals without a permit, and requires the removal of dogs

## Science and cooperation

W HEN international interest in Antarctica revived after World War II it was overshadowed by the tensions of the Cold War between the USA and the USSR. There was a danger that Antarctica itself could provoke confrontation between the super powers.

Alongside this political rivalry there has always been a strong thread of international scientific interest in the polar regions. This goes back to 1882–83 when the first International Polar Year focused interest on geomagnetic and auroral research (☛ p. 76). It was followed in 1932–33 by a second, and after the war a third polar year was proposed for 1957–58.

### International Geophysical Year

The International Council for Scientific Unions agreed to coordinate the research program, and the International Geophysical Year (IGY) became the largest scientific project ever undertaken. It had a special emphasis on meteorology, oceanography and geomagnetism in Antarctica.

Twelve nations set up 50 stations with a total of 5000 scientists and support staff to carry out the research program. America established five stations including Amundsen–Scott at the South Pole. Russia took up the even more difficult challenge of setting up Vostok station at the Pole of Inaccessibility, the point on the continent furthest from all its coasts. The stations were linked by a complex radio network. A weather centre was set up by the USA and staffed by meteorologists from seven nations.

*Australian scientists visiting the Russian base at Mirny.*

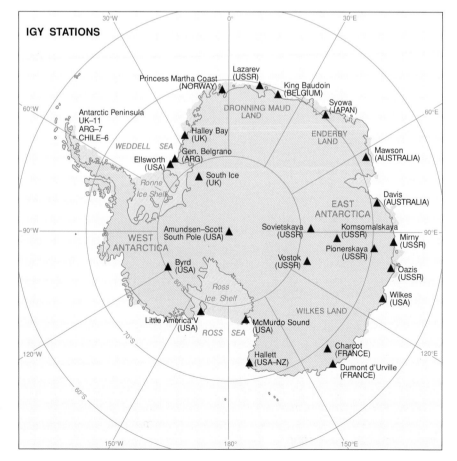

*Twelve nations established 50 stations in Antarctica for the International Geophysical Year in 1957–58. This set the pattern of stations of many different nations in all the seven territorial claims.*

## Transantarctic expedition

One of the most important achievements of the IGY was the fulfilment of Shackleton's earlier dream (☞ p. 36) to cross Antarctica from coast to coast. Vivian Fuchs followed almost the same plan but with Sno-cats and air support instead of dogs. He made the 3500 km journey from the Weddell to the Ross Sea via the Pole in 99 days. Edmund Hillary also reached the Pole from the Ross Sea, using converted Ferguson farm tractors.

The IGY was so successful in Antarctica that the Scientific Committee on Antarctic Research (SCAR) was set up to continue its work. SCAR has set up permanent working groups to coordinate research in eight areas of science. It also establishes groups of specialists to examine the scientific aspects of particular issues relating to science, conservation or operations. This provides a valuable input to the complex negotiations surrounding the various Conventions set up by the Treaty.

## BIOMASS program

For example, when CCAMLR was being negotiated, it was obvious that not enough was known to develop an effective ecosystem approach to conservation of marine resources. So SCAR organised the Biological Investigation of Marine Antarctic Systems and Stocks (BIOMASS).

In 1981 17 ships from eleven countries carried out a coordinated research program on the role of krill in the Antarctic ecosystem. One key project was the simultaneous sampling of krill populations all round the continent. This was done both by trawling, and by using echo sounding methods to locate and estimate the mass of krill swarms. All the data were analysed by the British Antarctic Survey and made available to all the 25 members of SCAR. No single country could have carried out such a huge research program. Only the cooperative spirit of SCAR made it possible.

The Commonwealth Transantarctic Expedition finally realised Shackleton's dream using 'tin dogs', like this converted Ferguson tractor.

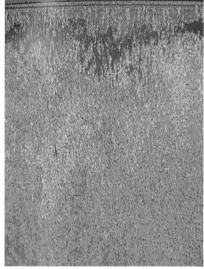

Echo sounding was first used during BIOMASS to locate and estimate the size of krill swarms. The swarm shows up as the orange mass at the top of the screen.

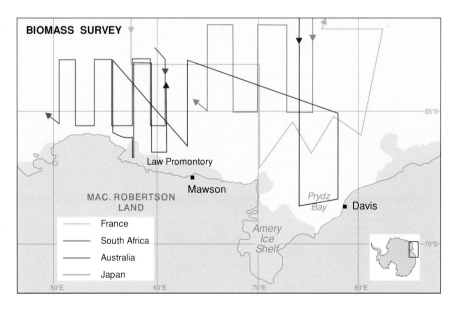

BIOMASS SURVEY

Law Promontory

Mawson

MAC. ROBERTSON LAND

Prydz Bay

Davis

Amery Ice Shelf

—— France
—— South Africa
—— Australia
—— Japan

Ships of several nations took part in the BIOMASS survey of Prydz Bay in West Antarctica.

Treaty members also run smaller joint projects in many areas of Antarctic science. Where several nations have stations close together they have frequent social contact as well. In addition, the better equipped nations like the USA and Russia willingly offer their icebreakers and aircraft to help ships in difficulty or for medical emergencies. So the cooperative spirit of Antarctic science extends far beyond research to many aspects of living and working on the continent.

# Tourism

**A** *VOYAGE to Antarctica retains the fascination and sense of adventure that the early explorers experienced when they first sailed to the 'last continent'. To witness Antarctica's majestic scenery is a privilege only a few are destined to experience.* **(Tourist brochure)**

More and more people are seeking this privilege. Does this mean that Antarctica is likely to be overrun by hordes of tourists who will injure its fragile ecosystems? Will more ships and aircraft mean a greater risk of oil spills, sinkings and crashes? How can tourism be managed so that more people do get the chance to enjoy the wonders of Antarctica without destroying them?

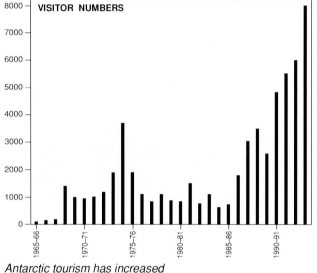

Antarctic tourism has increased rapidly in the last ten years.

## Visitor numbers

Antarctic tourism is not a mass market. Only around 50 000 tourists have ever visited Antarctica since the late 1950s when organised tourism began. It is increasing rapidly now, to about 8000 in 1993–94 (☛ graph).

Tourism tends to be concentrated in a few areas. The Antarctic Peninsula is by far the most popular region because the sea voyage is the shortest (☛ map on p. 70) and there are plenty of 'attractions' like seal and bird colonies and spectacular glaciers in a smaller area. This means that some popular spots may get several thousand visitors in a few months. A research team studying the impact of tourism on penguin and seal colonies on one island recorded 35 ship visits bringing over 3000 tourists over four months.

## Impact of tourism

Almost all tourists visit Antarctica by ship, and they go ashore only for brief periods so their impact is much less than that of permanent stations.

*Inflatable boats enable tourists to get a close up view of ice caves.*

*The Lemaire Channel on the Antarctic Peninsula is a spectacular cruising ground.*

For example, the 560 tourists who visited the Ross Sea sector in 1992–93 spent about 1000 person-days ashore. By comparison, the 1500 summer and 250 winter expeditioners at McMurdo and Scott bases in the same area totalled 200 000 person-days between them. Tourists do not drive vehicles, eat, sleep or generate waste while ashore, and their ships do not dump any garbage or sewage in the sea.

But even though they may leave nothing but footprints and take nothing but photographs, both these activities can be a threat to the Antarctic environment. Many moss beds on the Peninsula and offshore islands are so fragile that a single footprint can last for decades. To get that memorable shot, visitors may be tempted to approach too close to wildlife and disrupt breeding and nesting behaviour.

Tourism can also affect sites of human as well as natural interest. Historic buildings like the huts of early expeditions on Ross Island (☛ pp. 32–37) have been damaged by souvenir hunters, and even current stations are vulnerable. The psychological impact of a ship visit can be very disruptive on a close knit community (☛ p. 82), as well as interrupting work programs in the busiest period.

On the other hand, tourists make good ambassadors for Antarctica. Most already have a keen interest in the continent before they come, and take home an even greater commitment to its conservation.

## Future of tourism

In the future, the balance between positive and negative impacts of tourism will depend very much on how it develops. Ship-based tourism is the safest and least environmentally damaging. 'Flightseeing' — overflying without landing — can give more people a glimpse of the continent. Over 10 000 visitors enjoyed this opportunity in the 1970s until the fatal crash of a jumbo jet on Mt Erebus in 1979, and it has not resumed.

Although the Protocol gives priority to science, tourism is also a legitimate use of Antarctica's resources. There need not be any conflict between them, and in fact they could support each other, provided both adhere to the strict environmental standards required by the Protocol (☛ p. 93).

*Visits to penguin colonies are always popular, but can disrupt breeding habits.*

# The ozone 'hole'

THE ozone 'hole' was first identified in 1981 by British scientists working at Halley station in West Antarctica (☞ map p. 43). As a result of continuous measurements of ozone in the stratosphere since 1957, they detected a consistent decrease in ozone levels in springtime. This is one example of how Antarctic science contributes to our understanding of the environment of the planet as a whole.

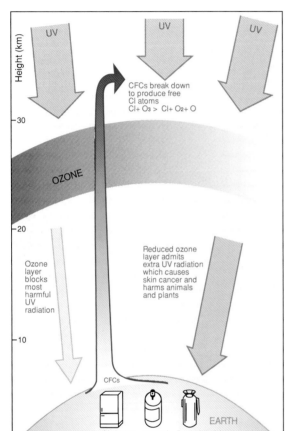

CFCs are carried into the stratosphere where they break down forming free chlorine atoms. These then sink into the ozone layer and break it up.

Ozone ($O_3$) is a gas made up of three atoms of oxygen, instead of the usual two that make up most of the oxygen ($O_2$) we breathe. Ozone is poisonous and, at low levels of the atmosphere, is a danger to life. But in the stratosphere, about 20 km above the ground, it forms a layer that protects all life on earth from the lethal effects of ultra-violet (UV) radiation. The amount of ozone in the atmosphere is minuscule — only about 0.00004%. So even a tiny change in this amount can have a dramatic impact.

## Ozone formation

Ozone is formed from oxygen by the action of sunlight and by electrical discharges like lightning. These processes are reversible, so that ozone in the stratosphere is constantly being produced and destroyed, but the level remains stable. However the scientists at Halley observed a 30% decrease in October ozone levels over ten years. In 1993 ozone reached a record low springtime level in Antarctica, about 70% below the level in the 1960s.

## CFCs

Research has proved that chemicals called CFCs (chloro-fluoro-carbons) are responsible for this rapid breakdown of ozone. CFCs are used in fridges and air-conditioners, plastic foams and aerosol sprays, and around 1 million tonnes are produced each year. CFCs are very stable compounds and can remain in the atmosphere for over 100 years. They are only broken down when they get high into the stratosphere, by ultra-violet radiation above the ozone layer. They release free chlorine atoms which in turn interact with ozone to break it down much more rapidly

Measurements at Halley base show that there has been little change in the ozone concentration in the autumn (right), while in spring (far right) it fell by more than 30% over ten years, with a more marked decrease every second year.

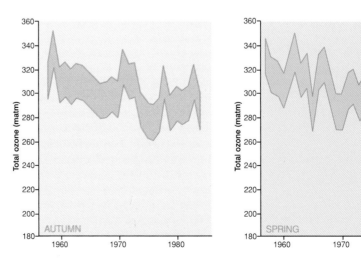

feedback loop is an example of how a change in one part of the system can affect other parts of interconnected systems, making modelling of climate change very complex.

*Scientists retrieve a gauge for measuring pressure at different ocean depths (left) and launch one for salinity and temperature measurements (above) on the Australian research ship Aurora Australis.*

## Biological systems

The biological systems of the Southern Ocean would be affected by, and would in turn influence, global warming in even more complex ways. The phytoplankton at the base of the food web (☞ pp. 46, 56), like all plants, absorb $CO_2$ and give out oxygen. Ocean warming would *increase* the quantity of phytoplankton which would absorb more $CO_2$, and so tend to *decrease* warming — an example of a *negative* feedback loop.

However, it is not quite as simple as this. Ocean warming would also mean less sea ice. This would reduce the area of the most productive zone, the seasonal sea ice zone (☞ p. 55). This would in turn cause an overall *decrease* in phytoplankton. Since less ice also means less vertical mixing in the ocean there would be less nutrients for phytoplankton. This would also *decrease* numbers and growth, and absorption of $CO_2$.

If there was also less wind due to interaction with the atmosphere, there would be less turbulence in the upper levels of the ocean and so phytoplankton would tend to sink more quickly. This would mean less food for krill and so reduce their numbers. Krill waste falling to the sea floor is one way in which carbon is transferred from the surface to the deep ocean. So fewer krill would also *decrease* absorption of $CO_2$. This sequence is a *positive* feedback loop, in which ocean warming *decreases* $CO_2$ absorption, which in turn *increases* warming.

There is another way in which the quantity of phytoplankton can affect global warming. They release sulphur compounds into the water which evaporate into the atmosphere. In reaction with other molecules these compounds form particles that act as cores on which water droplets condense in clouds. Clouds reflect sunlight and help keep the earth cool. So if ocean warming *increases* the quantity of phytoplankton, this would cause more cloud cover and tend to *decrease* the warming effect. This is another *negative* feedback loop.

# Global warming 3: The Antarctic ice sheet

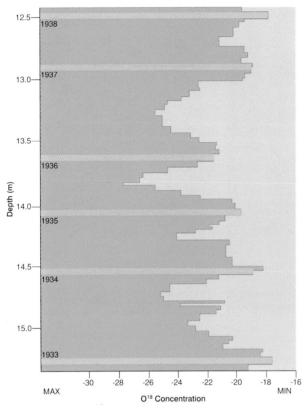

Analysis of the $O^{18}$ concentration can identify the annual layers in an ice core. The minimum levels of $O^{18}$ indicate the higher temperature of snow falling in summer. The distance between these layers shows the changing rate of annual accumulation. This record is from Dronning Maud Land.

THE Antarctic ice sheet holds some of the most important clues to the puzzle of global warming and its impact on the planet.

## History of the ice sheet

The ice sheet itself contains the history of climate change over the last few thousand years. By studying this record, scientists can identify the natural cycles in global warming and cooling (☛ pp. 12–13). This then makes it possible to estimate the impact of human induced changes on these natural cycles.

The present ice sheet is the result of slow accumulation of layers of snow compressed into firn then ice (☛ p. 23). Vertical cores drilled through several hundred metres provide a sample of all the layers which have accumulated over thousands of years, the oldest at the bottom. The deepest ice core so far drilled, near Vostok, reached 2500 metres and contains information from 230 000 years ago.

This information is of several kinds, based on analysing the composition of the water from which the ice is formed, the impurities in the ice, and the air trapped within it (☛ p. 23).

## Dating ice layers

First, it can be used to date the layers in the ice core. Snow and ice are both forms of water ($H_2O$) which can contain two types of oxygen atoms called $O^{18}$ and $O^{16}$. The concentration of these two types of oxygen atoms depends on the temperature of the snow when it fell. The lower the temperature, the less $O^{18}$ there is in the snow.

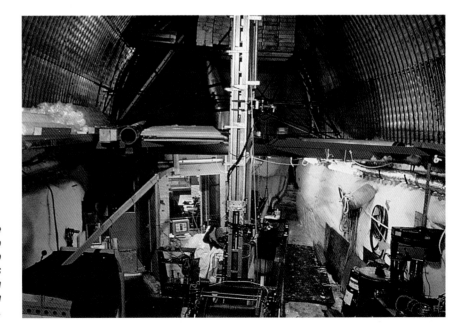

The ice drilling rig at Law Dome near Casey has a steel shelter to protect it and the scientists who operate it. A core 1200 metres deep to the bedrock was drilled in 1992-93, providing information from over 20 000 years ago.

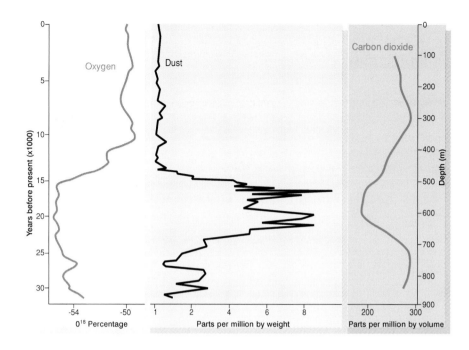

*This diagram shows evidence of changing temperature (from O$^{18}$ concentration) dust and CO$_2$ concentration over the past 30 000 years from a 900 metre deep core from the interior of East Antarctica. It shows that CO$_2$ and O$^{18}$ levels were both low during the last major ice age up to 15 000 years ago. There was also an abnormal amount of dust in the atmosphere. Then the O$^{18}$ level fell indicating the temperature rose, along with an increase in CO$_2$ concentration.*

By measuring the concentration of these two oxygen atoms, it is possible to tell if the snow fell in summer or winter, so that annual layers can be detected in an ice core. This is the simplest way to date a core, but it can only be used for short cores and time spans of up to 1000 years.

For deep cores scientists have to work out the ice flow dynamics at the site and calculate how long they would take to produce the layer structure found in the core. Many assumptions have to be made, so the deeper the core, the less accurate the dating.

## Concentration of atmospheric gases

Second, the air trapped in ice at different depths can be analysed to find the proportion of gases in the atmosphere at the corresponding time. Ice cores from Law Dome near Casey have given very precise information about increases in methane concentration in the past 200 years, and changes in CO$_2$ concentration can be traced for several thousand years.

In this way ice cores provide baseline data against which to measure current increases in greenhouse gases. They show that in the last major glacial period 10–20 000 years ago ( p. 13), both CO$_2$ concentration and temperature as measured by the O$^{18}$ concentration were low.

At the same time, there was a huge amount of dust in the atmosphere which was deposited in the ice. This implies that large areas of land in the southern hemisphere were very arid, with much more of the earth's water locked up in ice caps and glaciers.

Ice cores also show that the CO$_2$ concentration rose 30% at the end of the ice age and remained stable until 200 years ago. At the same time, the temperature rose. The precise relationship between changes in temperature and CO$_2$ concentration can be calculated from these data. This analysis suggests that the current rate of increase of CO$_2$ could produce a greater rate of global warming than any in the last 100 000 years.

Ice cores also show changes in the rate of snow accumulation, by the thickness of annual layers. This is critical for calculating the impact of global warming on the melting of the ice sheet.

*A scientist examines a section of the 10 cm diameter core.*

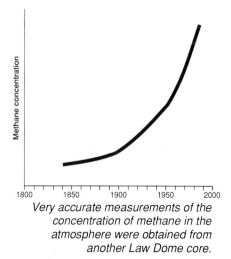

*Very accurate measurements of the concentration of methane in the atmosphere were obtained from another Law Dome core.*

## Global warming 4: Sea level rise

B Y STUDYING the history of climate change locked up in ice cores, glaciologists can supply information about the likely scale of global warming due to increases in greenhouse gases. From this and other evidence, they can also make predictions of the likely effect of global warming on the melting of the ice sheet.

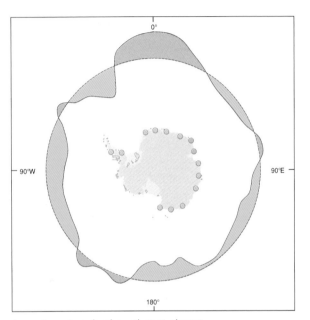

*Long term trends show that at almost all stations around the continent, the mean annual temperature is rising (yellow dots). It is falling at only a few places (blue dots). Similarly, the extent of sea ice is mostly decreasing (yellow areas) and is increasing in only a few places (blue areas).*

### Temperature rise and snow accumulation

Although it would seem logical that a rise in temperature would cause melting, that is unlikely to happen in the short term. In fact the most likely immediate effect will be increased accumulation, and this is already evident in the Law Dome core. The reason for this is that the interior of Antarctica is a desert, where very little snow falls, because the air is too cold to hold much water vapour (☛ p. 19). So an increase in air temperature will enable more water vapour to be carried inland, and to fall as snow, thus increasing accumulation.

### Melting of the ice sheet

Surface melting of the ice sheet only happens on a very limited coastal fringe during summer. The main cause of 'melting' is the flow of the whole mass of the ice sheet towards the sea, where it calves icebergs (☛ p. 26). The rate of flow depends on the temperature at the bedrock where the most rapid sliding occurs (☛ p. 24). But it would take many years for any temperature increase due to global warming to reach this level.

It is more probable that warmer ocean temperatures could weaken the attachment of floating ice shelves around the coast. This could cause huge sections — mega-icebergs — to break off, which would increase the gradient and rate of flow of glaciers feeding them. In this way, the total discharge of the ice sheet would increase.

*Surface melt streams in the ice sheet only flow for a short time in summer.*

However, at present the best estimates of the 'mass balance' of the ice sheet — that is, the difference between the rate of snow accumulation and loss through icebergs — suggest that it is positive. This means that the ice sheet is growing not shrinking. This in turn has been calculated to cause a drop in sea level of around 1 mm per year.

Since increased snow accumulation is the most likely immediate result of global warming, 'melting' of the Antarctic ice sheet will not make a major contribution to sea level rise. If the whole ice sheet were to melt it would raise the sea level by 60 metres. Melting of the ice shelves would produce a rise of 5 metres, but even this is unlikely.

*Melting of sea ice around the continent is the mostly likely short term effect of global warming in Antarctica.*

## Sea level predictions

The most rapid impact of global warming in the Antarctic region will be on pack ice formation. However, the main cause of sea level rise in the short term will be expansion of the oceans world wide because, like any material, water expands when it gets hotter.

The combination of ocean expansion with a reduction in sea ice, possibly some melting of ice shelves and a small positive mass balance of the Antarctic ice sheet, could cause a rise in sea level of up to 40 cm by 2030. This would be sufficient to inundate many coral atolls in the Pacific and Indian Oceans, and low-lying countries like Bangladesh.

While scientists try to find out more precisely how global warming will affect Antarctica and the Southern Ocean, all governments and countries need to do more to reduce greenhouse gas emissions to prevent even more drastic changes in climate and sea level.

*Coral atolls will be the most vulnerable to sea level rise due to ocean warming.*

# Glossary

'Apple' hut; red hemispherical fibreglass hut used by Australian field expeditions, which can be dismantled, or moved whole by helicopter; can also be expanded, by adding intermediate sections, to a 'Melon', 'Zucchini' or 'Cucumber'

auroras; moving streams or curtains of light, caused by interactions of charged particles from the sun with the outer fringes of the earth's atmosphere

blizzard; a combination of strong wind and blowing or falling snow

blubber; layer of fat under the skin and over the muscles which protects an animal from cold; can be eaten by humans

cold outbreak; sudden cold weather caused by very cold air from Antarctica being carried northwards over southern Australia

crevasse; deep cracks in the ice caused by ice movement

feedback loop; the effect of an outcome of a process on the process itself; either reinforcing it (positive) or decreasing it (negative)

firn; an intermediate stage in the conversion of snow to ice through accumulation

frostbite; inflammation of the skin, especially of the feet, face and hands, caused by exposure to extreme cold

glaciology; study of the formation, movement and evolution of ice

GPS; Global Positioning System—a system for fixing one's position on the earth's surface using a computer which calculates inputs from several satellite signals

Greenhouse effect; heating of the earth's atmosphere caused by increased levels of carbon dioxide, which prevents the escape of reflected solar energy

Hägglund; Swedish over-snow vehicle used on all Australian stations

'homers'; home brewed beer

'hoosh'; a very thick soup or stew, usually containing *pemmican*

hypothermia; very low body temperature, caused by prolonged exposure to extreme cold; can cause death

jollies; recreational excursions

katabatic wind; air mass which moves from the interior to the coast, down the slope under gravity

manhauling; sledge journey with people pulling the sledge

meteorite; fragment of rock which has reached the earth from outer space

meteorology; study of the atmosphere, especially for weather forecasting

ozone; a form of oxygen with three atoms in the molecule instead of two

pemmican; dried lean meat pounded into a paste with melted fat and pressed into cakes; used as field rations by early expeditions

plate tectonics; mechanism of continental drift, by which continents move very slowly towards or away from each other, carried on 'plates' floating on the earth's molten core

polynyas; areas of water in pack ice

quikes; four-wheeled agricultural motor bikes

'Red Sheds'; living quarters on Australian stations, named after the colour of the external panels of the buildings

sastrugi; wind-blown ridges on the surface of hard snow

scurvy; disease caused by vitamin C deficiency resulting from lack of fresh fruit and vegetables in the diet

seismic survey; calculating the thickness of an area of ice or rock by measuring the time taken for shock waves from special explosions to be reflected from different layers

snow blindness; loss of vision due to reflection of strong sunlight from snow or ice damaging the eyes

Sno-cats; early tracked over-snow vehicles

sundogs; bright spots or pillars of light around the sun, caused by refraction by ice crystals in the air

ventile; wind and snow-proof material used to make outer garments

whiteout; overcast conditions when the sky and the snow or ice surface merge without a horizon, making it almost impossible to judge distance or surface unevennesses

windchill; combination of wind and cold which lowers the apparent temperature

# Pictorial acknowledgements

Key: page number; t, top; m, middle; b, bottom; l, left; c, centre; r, right.

All maps and diagrams are drawn by AUSLIG, based on sources as specified.

**7** NRSC, **8ml** AUSLIG, **8b/9b** SPRI a, **9tl/tr** AUSLIG, **10tl** AGS, **10tr/11t** AGSO, **10mc** CUP, **10b/11b** AUSLIG, **11mr** P Quilty, **12l/13r** AGPS, **12bc** P Dombrovskis, **13tc** AAD/J Manning, **14** OUP/BAS, **15tr** AAD/J Hosel, **15mc** AAD/ R Garrod, **15br** AAD/R Tingey, **16tl** CUP, **16bl/br/17tc/bc** BOM, **17tr** AAD/M Higham, **17bc** AAD/D Watts, **18ml** CUP, **18mc** AUSLIG, **18bl/br/19bl/bc/br** BOM, **19tr** AAD/R Butler, **19mr** AAD/W Cannon, **20tl** BOM, **20ml** ACRC/ I Allison, **20bc** AAD/J Walter, **21tl/tr** BOM, **21mr** RD, **21bc** I Raymond, **22ml** AAD/G McInnes, **22tr** Dover Publications, **22bl/22bc** SPRI a, **23tc** ACRC/I Allison, **23mr** AGS, **23mc** ACRC/Li Jun, **24tl** SPRI a, **24mc** AAD/K Dalgleish, **24bl** LC, **25tr** ACRC/J Jacka, **25br** AAD/C Scott, **25mc** AAD/A Foster, **26ml/26mr** NASA, **27tr** AAD/D Luders, **27mr** AAD/ J Manning, **27bc** AAD/A Williams, **27br** LC, **28** NLA, **29** AGS, **30tl** ML, **30b** J Chester, **31** AGS, **32tr** AAD/H6143, **32bl** AGS, **33tr** ML, **33mc** AAD, **34bl** AGS, **34br** TMAG, **35tc** AAD/H5931, **35mr** AAD/H5033, **36tl** AAD/F Hurley, **36bl** NLA, **37tr** AAD, **37tc** NLA, **37br** WWN, **38tl** TEDM, **38b** AU, **39tr** ML, **39mr/bc** TEDM, **40l** AUSLIG, **40mc** AAD, **41** NLA, **42tl** GC, **42ml/bc** AG/D Smith, **43** AUSLIG, **44l** TEDM, **44mc** NGA, **45tc** NG, **45bc** J Senbergs, **45tr** SPRI b, **45br** AD/ H Ponting, **46bc/47bc** CUP, **46l** PP, **47r** GC, **48ml** FAO, **48bc** AAD/M Mallis, **49tr/bc** G Robertson, **50l** CUP, **50bc** AAD/ F Iliff, **51tr** LC, **51b** AAD/D Watts, **52ml** H Ling, **52mc** A Urie, **52mr** P Broady, **53tr** AAD/K Beinsson, **53tl** A Urie, **53mr** D Neilsen, **53bc** S Rando, **54ml/bc** CUP, **55tr** AAD/R Hahn, **55mc** AAD/R Bessor, **55mr** AAD/S Brookes, **56ml** AAD/ R Williams, **56bc** AAD/S Brookes, **57tc** AAD/H Marchant, **57br** AAD/S Rollins, **58tl** BBC, **58bl/mc** G Robertson, **59tc** RD, **59mr** AAD/R Butler, **59br** AAD/P Kilalea, **60tl** AUSLIG, **60bc** AAD/R Reeves, **61tc** AAD/R Morsan, **61br** AD/ S Brown, **62tl/bc** P Dombrovskis, **63mr** T Burridge, **63bc** TPWS, **64tl** TEDM, **64ml** NLA, **64bc** AAD/A Campbell Drury, **65tr** AUSLIG, **65mr** TEDM, **65bc** AAD, **66tl** AAD/G Merrill, **66bl** AAD/H Ponting, **66bc** LC, **67tr** AAD/G Snow, **67bc** TEDM, **68ml** ACS, **68bc** CM/H Ponting, **69tc** AAD/K Sheridan, **69mr** SPRI b, **69br** AAD/M Hesse, **70tl** C Douglas, **70ml** AAD/R Reeves, **70bc** AUSLIG, **71t** AAD/J Kelley, **71br** AAD/G Hoffman, **72tl** AAD/H Ponting, **72b** NLA, **73tc** AAD/ J K Davis collection, **73b** TEDM, **74tl** AAD/J Carr, **74mc** M Underwood, **74bl** LC, **75mr** AAD/M Corry, **75bc** LC, **76tl/bl** P Greet, **76mc** RD, **77tr** AAD/R Reeves, **77mc** AAD/P Sullivan, **78tl** LC, **78ml** AAD/G Else, **78bc** A Wenden, **79tr** T Diggins, **79mc** R Easther, **79br** P Dirks, **80tl** AAD, **80mc** AAD/R Reeves, **80bl** AAD/R Butler, **81tr** A Urie, **81mc** LC, **81br/82tl/bc** R Scott, **83mc** AAD/E Sworzak, **83br** D Patterson, **84tl** NLA, **84mc** AAD/P Law, **84bl** AAD/O Ertok, **85tr** LC, **85mc/br** AAD/G McInnes, **86bc** AAD/R Garrod, **87bc** CCAMLR, **88bc** AAD/R Wills, **89mr** CUP, **89bc** J Shevlin, **90ml/mr** CRES, **91mc** AAD, **92l** GC, **93tc** LC, **94ml** AAD/V Kamener, **94bc** AUSLIG, **95tr** NZAP, **95mr** AAD/S Brookes, **95bc** CUP, **96ml** SPRI c, **96bc/97tc/mr** S Campbell, **98ml/bc/br/99mr** A Plumb, **99mc/100 bl** CSIRO, **100tc** AUSLIG, **101tc** DFAT, **101ml/mr** AAD b, **102mc** AAD c, **103tc** AAD/M Betts, **103tr** AAD c/S Brookes, **104tl** AGS, **104bc** AAD/ G Snow, **105tc** RD, **105mr** J Chester, **105br** AAD c, **106tl** AAD c, **106bc** LC, **107tr** AAD/R Wills, **107bc** DFAT.

## Abbreviations

| | |
|---|---|
| AAD | Australian Antarctic Division |
| |   a Photographic Collection |
| |   b *ANARE News 65* |
| |   c *ANARE News 70* |
| ACRC | Antarctic Cooperative Research Centre |
| ACS | Australian Construction Services |
| AG | Australian Geographic/Dick Smith |
| AGPS | Australian Government Publishing Service, 1983 |
| AGS | American Geological Survey |
| AGSO | Australian Geological Survey Organisation |
| AU | Allen and Unwin, 1988, Jacka F & E (eds) *Mawson's Antarctic Diaries*, 399, 401 |
| AUSLIG | Australian Surveying and Land Information Group |
| BAS | British Antarctic Survey |
| BBC | British Broadcasting Corporation |
| BOM | Bureau of Meteorology |
| CCAMLR | Commission of Conservation of Antarctic Living Marine Resources |
| CM | Canterbury Museum, New Zealand |
| CRES | Centre for Resource and Environmental Studies, Australian National University, 1993, Handmer J &Wilder M (eds) *Towards a Conservation Strategy for the Australian Antarctic Territory*, 83 |
| CSIRO | Commonwealth Scientific and Industrial Research Organisation |
| CUP | Cambridge University Press, 1987, Walton D W H (ed) *Antarctic Science* |
| DASETT | Department of Arts, Sport, the Environment, Tourism and Territories *Impact of Climate Change* |
| DFAT | Department of Foreign Affairs and Trade |

| | |
|---|---|
| FAO | Food and Agriculture Organisation, 1985, Fischer W & Hureau J C (eds) *FAO species identification charts for fishery purposes, Southern Ocean* |
| GC | Greenpeace Communications, 1988, May J, *Greenpeace Book of Antarctica* |
| LC | Louise Crossley |
| ML | Mitchell Library, State Library of New South Wales |
| NASA | National Aeronautical and Space Administration |
| NG | Nolan Gallery, Collection: Estate of Sir Sidney Nolan |
| NGA | National Gallery of Australia |
| NLA | National Library of Australia |
| NRSC | National Remote Sensing Centre Ltd, United Kingdom |
| NZAP | New Zealand Antarctic Program |
| OUP | Oxford University Press, 1992, Tingey R (ed) *Geology of Antarctica* |
| PP | Pergamon Press, 1988, Bonner W N & Walton D W H, *Key Environments: Antarctica* |
| RD | Readers Digest, 1985, *Antarctica: Great Stories of the Frozen Continent* |
| SPRI | Scott Polar Research Institute |
| |   a 1983, Drewry, D J (ed) *Antarctica: Glaciological and geophysical Portfolio* |
| |   b Edward Wilson Collection |
| |   c 1992, *Polar Record 28* (164) 17-22, Enzenbacher D J 'Tourists in Antarctica: numbers and trends' |
| TEDM | Trustees of the Estate of the late Sir Douglas Mawson |
| TMAG | Tasmanian Museum and Art Gallery |
| TPWS | Tasmanian Parks and Wildlife Service |
| WWN | W W Norton and Co Inc, 1977, Worsley F A, *Shackleton's Boat Journey* |

# Index